FROM FIERCE TO FAITH

Healing and Renewal in Shakespeare's Women

Shakespeare for the Common Man
In Twelve Plays

By John Silver

Cover illustration: Judi Dench and Oliver Chris as Titania and
Bottom in *A Midsummer Night's Dream*. Photo courtesy of
Tristram Kenton. Graphic design by Jane Perkinson.

From Fierce to Faith, First Edition, 2015, published by Dryflier
Publishing Company.   ISBN 1516946014

Dedication

With undying love, this book is dedicated to Linda, my wife and partner, who suffers all my idiosyncrasies with a smile and always finds the right word or phrase when I am struggling and lost in a cloud. She is affection's avatar.

And to my kids, Erika, David, Maggie, Lincoln, and Jeff, who hung in there through thick and thin. Love surrounds us all.

I also remember some who are no longer here and others who are: My parents, Sylvia and John, who guided, nudged, and gave me every opportunity to live well and learn widely. To my sister, Grayce, always loving and encouraging. To Grandma Bella, the great woman of my youth, to special Aunt Tillie and Uncle Jack, and all my aunts, uncles, and cousins, unstinting in their support. To Walt Litz, my Princeton dorm neighbor, who tutored me on so many subjects for so many years. To Max Geffen, my first business boss, who trusted me to learn all his wisdom, day by day, and who financed my first venture.

Acknowledgements

Academia has been kind to me. Princeton's Larry Danson and Esther Schor ("Starry"), TCNJ's David Venturo (*il miglior fabbro*), David Blake, Jo Carney, Michael Robertson, Lincoln Konkle, and Lawrenceville's Champ Atlee, Mike Zuckerman, and Tom Absher, nurturers all. Irving Feldsott, who opened wide the door of theatre; Scott Ellsworth and Len Poliandro, who cajoled me into the public arena; Tyler Caton, Richmond Shreve, and Jane Perkinson, masters of technology, without whose help this book would simply take up space on my computer.

My love is as a fever, longing still
For that which longer nurseth the disease,
Feeding on that which doth preserve the ill,
Th' uncertain sickly appetite to please.
My reason, the physician to my love,
Angry that his prescriptions are not kept,
Hath left me, and I desperate now approve
Desire is death, which physic did except.
Past cure am I, now reason is past care,
And frantic-mad with evermore unrest;
My thoughts and my discourse as madmen's are,
At random from the truth vainly expressed:
For I have sworn thee fair, and thought thee bright,
Who art as black as hell, as dark as night.

Sonnet 147.

It is requir'd
You do awake your faith. Then all stand still:
Or – those that think it is unlawful business
I am about, let them depart....
Music, awake her; strike!
'Tis time; descend; be stone no more...
Dear life redeems you....
Her actions shall be holy....

The Winter's Tale

Table of Contents

Introduction: "Fascinating Rhythm":   6

What this book is and what it isn't.

Chapter One: "That's Why the Lady is a Tramp":   16

Joan of Arc in *1 Henry VI.*

Chapter Two: "You Do Something to Me":   32

From Juliet to Jessica: *Romeo and Juliet, A*

Midsummer's Night Dream, The Merchant of Venice.

Chapter Three: "They Didn't Believe Me": Women   92

in Wartime: *Troilus and Cressida, Antony and Cleopatra.*

Chapter Four: "My Funny Valentine": Women in   124

the High Tragedies: *Hamlet, Othello, King Lear, Macbeth.*

Introduction to Chapter Five   221

Chapter Five: "I'll Be Seeing You": The Miracle of   224

Rebirth: *The Winter's Tale* and *The Tempest*

Works Consulted   276

Appendix A: Chronology   283

Appendix B: Songs   287

INTRODUCTION

This book was born from another book, penned by a *provocateur.* In both his famous *Love and Death in the American Novel* and his less well known *The Stranger in Shakespeare,* Leslie Fiedler read at a thirty-degree angle. In the latter, Fiedler broached two related ideas that spawned my interest. After discussing the Moor as stranger (*Othello*) and the Jew as stranger (*The Merchant of Venice*), he then went on to say that the *real* stranger for Shakespeare was woman. "Obviously, the beginning for Shakespeare is the problem of woman, or, more exactly perhaps, his problem with women. Certainly, in his first plays, members of that sex are likely to be portrayed as utter strangers: creatures so

---

1. With apologies to the Gershwin brothers.

totally alien to men as [to] threaten destruction rather than offer the hope of salvation...."[2]

Fiedler's second, related notion dealt with daughters who turn their backs on their fathers. In Fiedler's reading of Shakespeare, daughters who cross their fathers are, by definition, witches and therefore must die. In Shakespeare, betraying daughters are not just here and there. "There is scarcely a play in the canon," he wrote, "in which daughters do not betray or seem to betray their fathers" (79). Fiedler cited Juliet, Desdemona, and Cordelia as daughters who forsake their fathers and die. This pattern begins early on, with Joan of Arc, in *1 Henry VI.* She is Shakespeare's avatar of a betraying daughter. In plain language she says to her father, who offers to die with her, "Thou art no father nor no friend of mine." And when she refuses to kneel for his blessing, father calls daughter a whore and then says to her and her English captors:

Dost thou deny thy father, cursed drab?

---

2. Leslie Fiedler, *The Stranger in Shakespeare*. New York, Barnes and Noble (1972), 43.

Oh, burn her, burn her! Hanging is too good.

(5.4.32-33)

Daughters who are witches, Fiedler went on, *must* die because that "grim biblical injunction never ceases to ring in Shakespeare's head: *A witch shall be put to death*"(80)! The grim injunction is from Exodus 22:18. In the Geneva Bible, which Shakespeare most probably knew, the verse reads, "Thou shalt not suffer a witch to live."[3] The passage is from the section of Exodus that prescribes all the rules governing daily life, in agonizing detail. Did Shakespeare really ponder all these proscriptions, alighting on 22:18 because it "rang" in his head? And can we label such women as Juliet, Desdemona, and Cordelia witches, and is the disavowal the *prime facie* cause of their deaths? I did not think so, even though witches, dark ladies, and the father-

---

3. All biblical quotations are from the 1599 edition of the *Geneva Bible*. White Hall, WV, Tolle Lege (2006). The Exodus passages should probably be read in the light of Deuteronomy 18 in which God specifies that only his anointed (or announced) prophets legitimately convey His words. This proscription bars such other mystics as soothsayers, sorcerers, or witches. If they presume to convey God's message, they must be "condemned to death" (Deut. 18:19-20).

daughter conundrum captured Shakespeare's imagination to the very end.

In his early and popular poem, *Venus and Adonis,* first printed in 1593, the poet very clearly depicts woman as stranger, as the "other." Venus has all the "equipment" to woo and win the beautiful young boy Adonis. After all, she is the goddess of love. But unlike Ovid's Adonis, Shakespeare's is not willing to play her erotic game. For him, her passion is suffocating, unalluring, and Adonis is afraid of her and the entire heterosexual encounter, a prequel to Bertram's fear of marital sexuality in *All's Well That Ends Well.*[4] For this Adonis, *One Touch of Venus* is one touch too many.[5] His rejoinder to her advances is, in effect: "Leave me alone. I just want to go hunting with my buddies."

---

4. See Richard Wheeler's intelligent and insightful discussion of *All's Well* in Chapter II, "Imperial Love and the Dark House" in his *Shakespeare's Development and the Problem Comedies: Turn and Counter-Turn*. Berkeley, UC Press (1981).
5. How ironic that 350 years later Marlene Dietrich dropped out of rehearsals for Kurt Weill and Ogden Nash's "One Touch of Venus," complaining that the show was "too sexy and profane." The show established Mary Martin, her replacement, as a new Broadway star. (Source = Wikipedia.)

Similarly, the Dark Lady of the sonnets brings the poet a bellyful of *angst;* he describes her as "black as hell, as dark as night" (Son. 147). He berates himself for succumbing to her sexual allure, which will "win me soon to hell"[6] (Son. 144). And then he must suffer the further injury when she also seduces his special friend, his "better angel," leaving him odd man out in this sexual *ménage a trois:*

> Two loves I have, of comfort and despair,
> Which like two spirits do suggest me still.
> The better angel is a man right fair,
> The worser spirit a woman colored ill.
> To win me soon to hell my female evil
> Tempteth my better angel from my side,
> And would corrupt my saint to be a devil,
> Wooing his purity with her foul pride.
>
> (Son. 144)

It's not a pretty picture, but I took comfort in the fact that this was early Shakespeare. I knew better days and better women would follow, like that rare Egyptian who "beggared all description," and, near the end of his

---

6. "Hell" both in the Dantean sense as well as pudendum, "Hell" in early Shakespeare.

career, magisterial Hermione, reborn from a celestial work of art.

Similarly, although I grieved with James, Joan of Arc's grossly dismissed father, I also knew more daughters would come – like young, lyrical Juliet, smitten by her father's enemy's son, like Desdemona, who "paragons description," like "the fair Ophelia," and like patient Cordelia, the epitome of paternal love. All of them die, as do Goneril, Regan, and Lady Macbeth. And then, as though by about 1610 all these dyings gave rise, phoenix-like, to redeeming daughters who could finally offer "the hope of salvation," Shakespeare treated us to singular Perdita, in *The Winter's Tale*, and wondrous Miranda, in *The Tempest*. One can only wonder why it took Shakespeare so long to acknowledge and embrace the unique gift only a daughter could bring to her father – the ability to create new life, a father's only hope for immortality.

My interest is rooted in the *stage depiction* of all these women. For me, they are all real women born of Shakespeare's imagination and transported to the stage as feminine characters, much as we see them in theatres worldwide today. We all know that in Shakespeare's day the women were played by young boys, skilled in their craft. This transvestite complication is fascinating to some but is not the subject of this book. When I read *Antony and Cleopatra*, I see in my mind's eye Elizabeth Taylor, Lynn Redgrave, or Harriet Walker and not a young boy actor dressed and made up to be the Queen of the Nile. In Hazlitt's words, "... you do not merely learn what his characters say, -- you see their persons... Each of his characters is ... as if they were living persons, not fictions of the mind."[7] The great actress Ellen Terry, who died in 1928, dubbed Shakespeare's women "these fearless, high-spirited, resolute and intelligent heroines."[8]

Nor will I address such questions as how Shakespeare came to know so well, as Phyllis Rackin

---

7. William Hazlitt, "On Shakespeare and Milton," Quoted in W.J. Bate, ed., *Criticism: The Major Texts.* New York, Harcourt Brace (1952), 307-308.
8. From an Ellen Terry lecture quoted in Isobel Armstrong's review of Gail Marshall's *Shakespeare and Victorian Women* in the August 14, 2009, *Times Literary Supplement*, 10.

tells us, "women's minds and hearts." Did leaving his wife behind in Stratford free him to get to know other women, and get to know them well, as the movie "Shakespeare in Love" infers? Did one of his daughters turn her back on him, embittering his soul? Legitimate and probably unanswerable questions, both beyond my scope. There are many splendid and recognized authors treading the feminist and historicist paths, all of them wielding more skillful pens than mine. My focus will remain narrow: *The play's the thing/ Wherein I'll catch* ... catch, I hope, something of the essence of the changes and development of Shakespeare's stage women.

There remains, then, one more question. If my subject is "From Fierce to Faith, Renewal in Shakespeare's Women," why begin with a history play? Fiedler's linkage of Joan in *1 Henry VI* to other daughters, even Cordelia, was a starting point. But more generically, Shakespeare's history plays deal with more than a dramatization of real events described by such chroniclers as Raphael Holinshed and Edward Hall. As Rackin observed, "history is not simply a record of heroic names and glorious deeds …: it is also a *connected story*, tracing the passing down of land and titles from one man to another and validating the legitimacy of their current apportionment."[9]

Likewise, I will attempt to assay whether what Shakespeare created in the character of Joan of Arc, *la Pucelle,* was born in the sonnets (or the other way around; see footnote 16) and also initiates a "connected story" involving Juliet, Cleopatra, Cordelia and other great stage women. In his "Preface to Shakespeare," Samuel Johnson reminds us, "In the writings of other poets a character is too often an individual; in those of *Shakespeare* it is commonly a species."[10] I have dared use "Shakespeare for the Common Man" as my subtitle to indicate that I am not an academic. There are no initials after my name. Although footnotes and references (some of them ridiculously arcane) are sprinkled through this book, I write as a common man for common men and women. As an example, in the

---

9. Phyllis Rackin, "Anti-Historians: Women's Roles in Shakespeare's Histories," *Theatre Journal.* 37.3 (1985),336. Italics mine.
10. Bate, 209.

Romeo and Juliet chapter, I describe Juliet's famous "O Romeo, Romeo, wherefore art thou Romeo?" (2.2.33) to mean, "Hey, dude, we have a name problem."

Although the discrepancies are minor, scholars do not always agree on the chronology of Shakespeare's poems and plays. I have used Harold Bloom's, both because his was handy and because I have always respected his scholarship. I have reproduced his basics listing in Appendix A, from his *Shakespeare: The Invention of the Human.* To Bloom's chronology I have added a few significant dates gleaned from a Folger Library listing. The reasons behind joining song titles to chapter headings are detailed in Appendix B, "Songs."

With luck, the rhythmic articulation of the women you are about to meet will fascinate and please you as much as the Gershwin brothers music does.

CHAPTER I. Joan of Arc in *1Henry VI*

Glory is like a circle in the water,
Which never ceaseth to enlarge itself
Till by broad spreading it disperse to nought.

If Joan *la Pucelle* in *1 Henry VI* is the avatar of the betraying daughter, where did she come from? In this earliest of Shakespeare's history plays, did Shakespeare invent her simply to vent his spleen against daughters who turn their backs on their fathers? Or was it to demonstrate to his English audience that not even a saintly heroine can save the French when fighting the English? He found Joan alive and well in his sources, Raphael Holinshed and Edward Hall.

From Holinshed we learn that Joan was 18 years old, that her father, James, was "a sorry shepherd" (lower class), that her mother's name was Isabel, and that she was "likesome" (agreeable or pleasant), courageous, politically astute ("an understander of

---

11. With apologies to Rodgers and Hart.

councils"), and chaste "both of body and behavior." In battle she was "mustered as a man" and "fought and did many slaughters by her own hands." She convinced the Dauphin that she was guided by "revelation divine" and would lift the English siege of Orleans and "drive the English out of the country."[12]

As we might expect, there are significant differences between Holinshed's and Shakespeare's Joan. Holinshed relates at least two versions of Joan's capture and death. In one version, a French lover, Guillaume de Flavie, sold her to the Lord of Luxembourg, one of whose followers then re-sold her to the English "for ten thousand pounds in money and three hundred pounds rent." Then the English "for witchcraft and sorcery burnt her at Rouen." According to this version, the English were willing to pay a high price to get rid of their "scourge." It's tempting to wonder why Shakespeare did not massage this version and perhaps even compare it to Judas's betrayal for thirty pieces of

---

12. Raphael Holinshed, *Chronicles of England, Scotland, and Ireland* (1587. 1429: 1.2). From the *Signet edition of 1 Henry VI*. New York, New American Library (2005), 146-147.

silver. Perhaps Joan's being French prohibited this kind of metaphoric sally.

In another version, the French condemned her as a witch and burned her. An inquiry by the Bishop of Beauvais revealed that Joan had acted and dressed like a man, a clear anti-social signal, and had become "a pernicious instrument ... in devilish witchcraft and sorcery." In this version Joan attempted to stave off execution by claiming to be pregnant, but without naming names, as she does in *1 Henry VI* (5.4.60ff). Not surprisingly, the French were willing to give her the benefit of the doubt and stayed execution for nine months. But eight days later "was she thereupon delivered over to secular power, and so executed by consumption of fire in the old market place at Rouen ... her ashes afterward without the town walls shaken into the wind...."[13]

In neither Hall nor Holinshed is there any confrontation between Joan and her father or any denial by Joan of her patrimony. In his compilation of

_____

13. Holinshed. 1430-31: 5.3,4 (pp. 149-151 in Signet).

Shakespeare's sources, Geoffrey Bullough comments that Joan "goes far beyond anything found in Hall or Holinshed."[14] Not surprisingly, then, the showdown scene is pure Shakespeare. Not only is it riveting drama, but it also evinces Shakespeare's early attraction to dissecting what is conventional, especially when satire is his major mode. A daughter denying her father? And the father turning her over to the enemy, with an injunction to burn her at the stake?[15] In addition to its dramatic quality, Joan's disavowal is consistent with Elizabethan patrilineal beliefs. Shakespeare dramatized them with a grin in *The Taming of the Shrew* and grimly in *King Lear*.

One may, however, inquire: Why use Joan for such a demonstration? Shakespeare's root reason for Joan's puissance in battle is to dramatize how dissension at home and cowardice in battle lead to the loss of all that the great Henry V accomplished in France. Early in the

14. Quoted in Gabriele Bernhard Jackson's "Topical Ideology: Witches, Amazons, and Shakespeare's Joan of Arc," Chapter 8 in Deborah Barker and Ivo Kamps, eds, *Shakespeare and Gender*. London, Verso (1995), 142.
15. We see a faint shadow of this in *Troilus and Cressida* when Cressida's father, Calchas, delivers her to the Greek enemy in the person of Diomedes with an indifferent, "She comes to you" (5.2.5).

play, Henry VI, despite his youth, lectures his nobles and pinpoints the obvious moral:

> Civil dissension is a viperous worm
> That gnaws the bowels of the commonwealth.
> (3.1.72-3)

Of all the English commanders, only Lord Talbot, who places king and country above personal gain, fights well in the field. He is the great English hero of *1 Henry VI*, defeated only when Somerset and York allow their personal feud to delay his rescue. As Lucy tells Somerset:

> The fraud of England, not the force of France,
> Hath now entrapped the noble-minded Talbot;
> Never to England shall he bear his life,
> But dies betrayed to fortune by your strife.
> (4.4.36-9)

Talbot's gallant young son, John, refuses to leave his father's side, even though both know they are hopelessly surrounded with no English help forthcoming. They are "betrayed … by [English] strife." With his dead son in his arms, Talbot gives up the ghost in a beautiful male *pieta* scene, foreshadowing the forlorn father-daughter *pieta* at the end of *King Lear.*

But something else lurks beneath the surface. In the very first scene in France, Act 1, Scene 2, Joan is brought to the Dauphin's military headquarters by Jean, Count Dunois, the Bastard of Orleans, suggesting that something unnatural is afoot. The Dauphin and Reignier unsuccessfully try to trick Joan, who brazenly tells them, "There's nothing hid from me." The reason, she explains, is that "God's mother deigned to appear to me," and henceforth Joan claims the wisdom and protection of the Virgin Mary. Before Joan has a chance to show her manly battlefield mettle, she reveals that the Virgin miraculously and symbolically changed her appearance:

> In complete glory she [the Virgin] revealed herself;
> And, whereas I was black and swart before,
> With those clear rays which she infused on me
> That beauty am I blessed with which you may see.
> (1.2.83-6)

"Black and swart before." Joan is the Dark Lady of the sonnets[16] whose irresistible sexuality entraps both the poet and his beloved, just as Joan ensnares the Dauphin and who knows how many others of his retinue.

That Joan is a witch Shakespeare makes clear, not just because she is so labeled by Talbot and York. In 5.3, the tide of battle turns decisively against the French, who flee before York's advancing troops, gallantly abandoning *la Pucelle.* In desperation, she invokes her guiding spirits, her "speedy helpers, that are substitutes/ Under the lordly monarch of the north [i.e., the Devil]," and Shakespeare brings them onstage, in a colorful prequel to *Macbeth's* weird sisters. They are called "Fiends." The stage directions tell us that they "walk and

---

16. Or the other way round: the Dark Lady of the sonnets is Joan. We latter day amateurs tend to think of the sonnets as all of a piece, as though one day Shakespeare sat down and said, "Today, I'll write my sonnets." Scholars believe that Shakespeare wrote *Venus and Adonis* and *Lucrece* in 1592-4, when the theatres were closed for most of those two years and probably also wrote many of the sonnets sometime in the 1590s. John Velz (in *The Shakespeare Newsletter,* Spring/Summer 2008) notes that "the sonnet fashion was declining by the late 1590s" and that during the plague years Southampton was being pressured by his family to marry. In his *Shakespeare, The Invention of the Human,* Harold Bloom dates *1 Henry VI* before the sonnets. I'm happy either way.

speak not," then "hang their heads," then "shake their heads," without speaking – that is, they perform a dumb show as their way of denying Joan's plea for otherworldly assistance. Finally, "They depart." Poor Joan!

Joan does her best to conjure them for assistance, offering first her blood, then one of her limbs, then her entire body, and – finally – her soul: "Then take my soul; my body, soul, and all,/ Before that England give the French the foil." Her Faustian offer avails her not:

> See, they forsake me! ....
> My ancient incantations are too weak,
> And hell too strong for me to buckle with.
> Now, France, thy glory droopeth to the dust.
> (5.3.24-9)

The Faustian flavor of this scene is clear. What is not so clear to Thomas Merriam is who wrote the episode. Merriam claims that in Joan's invocation to her spirits, her phrase "aid me in this enterprise" (5.3.7) appears nowhere else in Shakespeare or in Elizabethan verse drama except in Marlowe's *Doctor Faustus* (the 1616 version) at 4.2.10. His conclusion is either that Marlowe contributed this scene or that Shakespeare heard it in a performance and simply filched the line. Both dramas were presumably written and/or performed in 1592. Either way emphasizes Joan's diabolical bargain, and Merriam's brief note is well worth reading.[17]

In its day, *1 Henry VI* was a roaring success. In an article about Joan, Carole Levin cites reasons why Thomas Nash's 1592 estimate that at least ten thousand spectators saw the play is probably low; the figure, she believes, is most likely closer to twenty thousand.[18] Now no one reads the play except besotted graduate students and their besworn professors. Perhaps one reason the play was so popular was that Shakespeare's audiences warmed to Joan and heard familiar echoes. The Bastard introduced her to the Dauphin as a wondrous prophetess:

> The spirit of deep prophecy she hath,

---

17. Thomas Merriam. "Faustian Joan." *Notes and Queries* 49.2 (June 2002), 218-220.
18. Carole Levin. "'Murder not then the fruit within my womb': Shakespeare's Joan, Foxe's Guernsey Martyr, and Women Pleading Pregnancy in Early Modern English History and Culture." *Quidditas: Journal of the Rocky Mountain Renaissance Association* 20 (1999), 78.

Exceeding the nine sybils of old Rome.
What's past and what's to come she can descry.
(1.3.34-6)

Albert Tricomi explains how that claim was bound to set off Elizabethan alarm bells since prophesying or divination was deemed a sure signal of sorcery, a sally straight from the Devil.[19] On July 19, 1559, thirty some-odd years prior to the play's production, Queen Elizabeth had issued a proclamation warning her people against using any enchantments and had established a commission of enforcement. Injunction 460 read, in part, "that no person shall use charms, sorcery, enchantments, witchcrafts, soothsaying, or any like devilish device, nor shall resort at any time to the same for counsel or help."[20]

In the play, the English, primarily Talbot, York, and Warwick, mercilessly taunt Joan and view her claim to piety as a parody, perhaps reminding Shakespeare's

---

19. Albert H, Tricomi. "Joan la Pucelle and the Inverted Saints Play in 1 Henry VI." *Renaissance and Reformation* XXV, 2 (2001), 11.
20. Paul L. Hughes and James F. Larkin. *Tudor Royal Proclamations*, Vol. II. New Haven, Yale UP (1969), 117ff.

Protestant audiences of the many parodies of fraudulent Catholic ceremonies in plays by John Bale[21] and others. Theatrical attacks on Rome were one feature of popular dramas at universities as well as on public stages.[22]

One may also wonder to what extent Shakespeare's Joan reminded Shakespeare's audiences of Shakespeare's Queen. Elizabeth was widely known as The Virgin Queen and the Warrior Queen. One of Joan's French suitors, the Duke of Alençon was also one of Elizabeth's suitors. To see Joan on stage wearing battle-ready armor must have reminded Shakespeare's audiences of their military Queen wearing manly armor at Tilbury in 1588, when fear of a Spanish invasion was at its height. Elizabeth's speech to the assembled troops was one of her most famous:

I have always so behaved myself that, under God, I have placed my chiefest strength and safeguard in the loyal hearts and good will of my subjects…. I am come amongst you … resolved, in the midst and heart of the

---

21. Tricomi mentions three such Bale plays: "The Knaveries of Thomas Becket" (c. 1536-39, now lost)," King Johan" (1538), and "Three Laws" (c. 1548).
22. Cf. Tricomi's discussion, 8-13.

battle, to live or die amongst you all …. I know I have the body of a weak and feeble woman, but I have the heart and stomach of a King, and of a King of England too, and think foul scorn that Parma or Spain or any Prince of Europe should dare to invade the borders of my realm.[23]

In tone and resolve, if not in exact words, Elizabeth sounds much like Joan, both women partaking of the Elizabethan fascination with Amazons and warrior- and cross-dressing women. The resemblance may very well have prompted Shakespeare to insert the Faustian scene described above in order to assure his audience (and the censor) that similarities notwithstanding, Elizabeth was not Joan and that Joan was, after all, a French witch. In addition, at just the time *1 Henry VI* was playing in London (about 1591-92), once again English forces were in France, led by the charismatic Essex. Indeed, many playgoers saw Talbot as a stage proxy for him.[24]

---

23. From Carole Levin, *The Reign of Elizabeth I*. New York, Palgrave (2002), 70.
24. See Jackson's more thoroughgoing description of the similarity (footnote 14).

When Joan is captured by the English, to avoid being executed she claims pregnancy and demands her common-law right: "Then, Joan, discover thine infirmity, / That warranteth by law to be thy privilege./ I am with child …. (5.4.60-62)[25] This claim, too, would resonate with Shakespeare's audiences, as "pleading pregnancy was a familiar part of the justice system in England in the medieval and early modern period."[26] In addition, many Elizabethans owned copies or were familiar with John Foxe's widely distributed *Acts and Monuments,* commonly known as *The Book of Martyrs*, which detailed the execution of accused women "whose exemplary behavior, usually at the stake, defined the hallmarks of the true saints … of the new Reformed Church." The similarity between how Joan faced death with how Anne Askew, "the preeminent female martyr in Foxe," must have reverberated with Elizabethans and helped make *1 Henry VI* such a popular entertainment.[27]

---

25. Precisely the claim, so many years and plays later, that saved the foul witch Sicorax's life in Algiers. See *The Tempest*, 1.2.269-70.
26. Levin, 76.
27. Cf. Tricomi's discussion, 7-9.

Barbara Hodgdon goes even farther, commenting that "Joan represents a subversive challenge to gender," whose image echoes that of the Queen and who functions as "a spectacular, and intensely troubling, site of gender display."[28] In referencing Hodgdon, Levin cites rumors of sexual misconduct by Elizabeth, of hidden pregnancies, and even of "babies being burned alive." In the 1580s, she writes, Dionisia Deryck and Robert Gardner (two contemporaries) were severely punished for claiming that the Queen's bastard children were burned as infants.[29] Playgoers who paid close attention would also remember that Joan herself was a bastard. When Joan denies her father, he responds, "I did beget her, all the parish knows;/ Her mother liveth yet, can

---

28. Barbara Hodgdon, *The End Crowns All: Closure and Contradiction in Shakespeare's History.* Princeton, PU Press (1991), 55, cited in Levin, 77.
29 Levin, 77. Also, see the redoubtable Levin's chapter, "Gender, Monarchy, and the Power of Seditious Words" in Julia M. Walker, ed. *Dissing Elizabeth: Negative Representations of Gloriana.* Durham, Duke U Press (1998), esp. pp. 90-91. The general outcry and specific laws passed against infanticide may have played a role in assisting Leontes's courtiers in convincing him not to burn his new-born daughter. See *The Winter's Tale*, 2.3.155-157.

testify/ She was the first fruit of my bachelorship" (5.4.11-13).

Here is Coppélia Kahn's laconic summary: "As virgin prophetess, mannish Amazon, and seductive courtesan, Joan is a composite portrait of the ways women are dangerous to men."[30] And so was the Dark Lady. Early on, some deep instinct told Shakespeare that dramatically and thematically *unconventional* was more interesting than *conventional* and that the Dark Lady of his sonnets was too powerful a figure, a kind of "perturbed spirit," to rest only in his highly stylized Elizabethan prosody. As Salisbury is dying, a messenger tells Talbot that the Dauphin has entered the lists, accompanied by Joan *la Pucelle.* His rejoinder: "Frenchmen, I'll be a Salisbury to you./ Pucelle or pussel, Dolphin or dogfish,/ Your hearts I'll stamp out with my horse's heels,/ And make a quagmire of your mingled brains." (1.4.106-109) And so, from the quagmire of this early history play, Joan emerges as a puzzle, or a *pucelle,*

---

30. Coppélia Kahn, *Man's Estate: Masculine Identity in Shakespeare.* Berkeley, UC Press (1981), 55, Cited in Tricomi, 13.

or a puzzel and sometimes all three. Like Shakespeare's Dark Lady, Joan does not disappear from the canon. She will reappear, as a faint echo with pregnant Sycorax, in all Shakespearean daughters who turn away or seem to turn away from their fathers, and in all her hellish splendor as Lady Macbeth.

CHAPTER II. From Juliet to Jessica
Romeo and Juliet, A Midsummer Night's Dream, The Merchant of Venice

■ *Romeo and Juliet*

> Come gentle night, come loving black-brow'd night,
> Give me my Romeo; and when I shall die
> Take him and cut him out in little stars,
> And he will make the face of heaven so fine
> That all the world will be in love with night,
> And pay no worship to the garish sun.

The key question *Romeo and Juliet* poses is this: Does Juliet have a chance? For make no mistake, despite its title, this famous love-drama is Juliet's story.[32] Does she have a chance to engender a healthy, reciprocal relationship of love and trust with her father who, almost simultaneously, represents what is best and what is worst in this ancient, walled enclave? And if so, does she have a chance, along with Romeo, to break free

---

31. With apologies to Cole Porter.
32. As the Prince affirms, in the play's closing lines: "For never was a story of more woe/ Than this of Juliet and her Romeo."

from the family's tie to its primal feud, a grudge vendetta that threatens the lovers' freedom as well as the city's polity?

Joan of Arc admitted no discourse with James, her father, even though he offered the supreme Christian sacrifice: "Greater love than this hath no man, when any man bestoweth his life for his friends" (John 15:13). Is Juliet, then, a more refined Joan of Arc, four years younger, born anew in Italy, and truly a virgin? Knowing that in the end Juliet dies, we should first ask whether she disavows her father, Old Capulet, following the pattern of Joan *la Pucelle*. Because of her firm resolve not to marry Paris, her father's unyielding choice, Shakespeare shows us Capulet turning his back on Juliet, not the other way around.[33] They are the two characters who change the most in the play, and they represent Shakespeare's early take on the father-daughter relationship.

---

33. Marianne Novy has written that fathers rejecting daughters is the predominant pattern, not Fiedler's other way round. See her "Shakespeare and Emotional Distance in the Elizabethan Family," Chapter 4 in Barker and Kamps.

In the beginning, Juliet is a young, dutiful daughter. In 1.3, to her mother: "Madam, I am here. What is your will?" And when Lady Capulet raises the subject of marriage, Juliet responds, "But no more deep will I endart mine eye / Than your consent gives strength to make it fly." What more could an Elizabethan mother ask for? But this is before she meets Romeo, before they share a sonnet whose concluding couplet is a kiss, and before they exchange an Edenic kiss in the garden. Her newly released passion helps her mature quickly and push her, willy-nilly, toward parental confrontation. In this sense, Juliet reflects a long tradition, extending back before the Brothers Grimm, "in which it is necessary for the young girl to rebel against her father so she can move from daughterhood to wifehood."[34]

The famous balcony scene, 2.2, reveals critical differences between the two young lovers. Hidden in the Capulet garden, Romeo begins by comparing Juliet to the sun, then her two eyes to two stars, and then to a

---

34. See Jo Eldridge Carney, *Fairy Tale Queens*. New York, Palgrave Macmillan (2010), Chapter Four, especially 71.

bright angel sailing "upon the bosom of the air." (2.2.2-32). His entire 30-line recitation features images of praise that a painter might use to describe his portrait of a beautiful young woman. We would not have been surprised to hear Romeo utter (filching from Sonnet 18), "Shall I compare thee to a summer's day?" It's very fanciful stuff.

Juliet, on the other hand, wastes no time tackling the overriding problem the kids must now face, starting in line 33 of 2.2: "O Romeo, Romeo, wherefore art thou Romeo?/ Deny thy father and refuse thy name./ Or if thou wilt not, be but sworn my love/ And I'll no longer be a Capulet." No fanciful, stuff for her. "Hey, dude, we have a name problem."

Juliet does not know she is being overheard, so she goes on, just to herself, with her famous couplet (in ll. 43-4), "What's in a name? That which we call a rose/ By any other word would smell as sweet...." Her solution to the name problem involves a simple exchange (in ll. 47-9): "Romeo, doff thy name,/ And for thy name, which is no part of thee,/ Take all myself." Could it be any clearer? "Take all myself." Juliet is on the cusp of womanhood, preparing to abandon Elizabethan rules of patriarchy, choose her mate on her own, and give herself to Romeo wholeheartedly.

When Romeo reveals himself, although Juliet is surprised, she is down-to-earth, asking VERY practical questions: "How'd you get here? Do you have a GPS? How'd you know where I live? How'd you scale these high orchard walls? Don't you realize how dangerous it is? If my kinsmen find you, they will kill you." And how does Romeo respond? As though he's in a Peter Pan theatrical playhouse, where love conquers all with the wave of a wand. Not one of his answers speaks to Juliet's pragmatic queries. She's in one place, he's in another. What's clear is that she wants to continue this wooing conversation because she knows where she wants it to go. Yet, deep inside, pragmatic Juliet also fears their romance is heading for big trouble: "Although I joy in thee,/ I have no joy of this contract tonight: It is too rash, too unadvis'd, too sudden,/ Too like the lightning, which doth cease to be/ Ere one can say 'It lightens.'" (2.2.116-120) It's typical Shakespearean foreshadowing, alerting us to several grim roadblocks the two youngsters must soon face.

Romeo does not respond to her bolt of lightning. Instead, he pushes the conversation toward the edge of the balcony by asking (in l. 125): "O wilt thou leave me so unsatisfied?" As though that was all Juliet had to hear, she advances their chess game to its conclusion. First, this pledge: "My bounty is as boundless as the sea,/ My love as deep: the more I give to thee/ The more I have, for both are infinite." (ll. 133-35) And finally:

> Three words, dear Romeo, and good night indeed.
> If that thy bent of love be honourable,
> Thy purpose marriage, send me word tomorrow ...
> And all my fortunes at thy foot I'll lay,
> And follow thee my lord throughout the world.
> (2.2.142-8)

Married in secret, Juliet anticipates her wedding night with a passionate soliloquy fusing "sexual ecstasy and extinction"[35]:

> Come gentle night, come loving black-brow'd night,
> Give me my Romeo; and when I shall die
> Take him and cut him out in little stars,
> And he will make the face of heaven so fine
> That all the world will be in love with night,
> And pay no worship to the garish sun. (3.2.20-5)

Juliet is now speaking lines as beautiful and meaningful as any Shakespearean woman up to this point in his stage career. We may not hear anything more radiant until Cleopatra's last scene. It is Juliet who proposes marriage, a singularly unconventional posture, especially in Elizabethan times. Does it provide one more signal of Shakespeare's growing interest in women who can think for themselves?

In *The Merchant of Venice*, perhaps only one year after *Romeo and Juliet*, there is no question that Portia outclasses all the men, from Shylock to Antonio and certainly to her lover, Bassanio. In *Twelfth Night*, five or

---

35. Gibbons, 65.

six years later, in the end Viola gets her man through sheer bravura, but she has to pretend to be a man right up to the final recognition scene. Closing out his solo career with *The Tempest* in 1611, about a decade and a half after *Romeo and Juliet*, Shakespeare invents a kind of mother earth young woman, Miranda, who suddenly meets Ferdinand, heir to the throne of Naples and – ironically – the son of her father's enemy. We see another young couple struck by Cupid with love at first sight. And once again, the woman proposes to the man. Midway through the play, after mutual declarations of love, it is Miranda who pops the question:

> Hence, bashful cunning,
> And prompt me, plain and holy innocence!
> I am your wife, if you will marry me.... (3.1.81-3)

Juliet's passion, including her marriage proposal, has to survive the news that Romeo has killed her cousin Tybalt.[36] Although she is at first unsettled, Juliet remains true to her core. And when (in 3.5) her mother speaks

---

36. Despite the similarity of their names, Tybalt bears no resemblance and is not Talbot (from *1Henry VI*) reborn.

about wreaking vengeance on Romeo for killing Tybalt, Juliet speaks a femininely mature double language that her mother cannot possibly understand:

> O, how my heart abhors
> To hear him [Romeo] nam'd, and cannot come to him
> To wreak the love I bore my cousin [Tybalt]
> Upon his body that hath slaughter'd him.
>   (3.5.99-102)

This young Juliet is well on her way to becoming Cleopatra, early in her creator's career.[37]

In the beginning, old Capulet is a thoughtful, caring father. In his first scene with Paris (1.2), he tells Juliet's aristocratic suitor that she is too young for marriage; Paris should hold off for another two years: "My child is yet a stranger to the world... / Let two more summers wither in their pride / Ere we may think her ripe to be a bride." Capulet goes so far as to tell Paris that first he has to win Juliet, for "her consent is but a part, /And she agreed, within her scope of choice / Lies my consent and fair according voice." How many

---

37. Sadly, both women commit suicide.

Elizabethan fathers would tell a potential suitor that their daughters have a choice in the matter of matrimony? Three scenes later, at the Capulet's masked ball, he is the perfect host, even when told by his hot-tempered nephew that young Romeo, a Montague, has crashed the party:

> Content thee, gentle coz, let him alone,
> A bears him like a portly gentleman;
> And, to say truth, Verona brags of him
> To be a virtuous and well-govern'd youth.
> I would not for the wealth of all this town
> Here in my house do him disparagement. (1.5.64-9)

How ironic that the only information about Romeo's street reputation comes from Old Capulet, and perhaps doubly ironic that Capulet calls him "well-govern'd" when Romeo will so soon disparage the Capulet family by ungovernly killing Tybalt. How modern Old Capulet seems here, how far from the Elizabethan convention of Father Knows Best.

Then why does Old Capulet change his mind so radically? It is a key question whose answer bears on Shakespeare's thinking about this parent and this

41

daughter in this walled city of Verona. In his second meeting with Paris (3.4), Capulet urges a quick marriage, even though he admits that he and Lady Capulet have had little time to discuss the match with Juliet. Is Paris so eloquent and convincing that Capulet gives way? To the contrary. Paris was about to take his leave and said only "Commend me to your daughter," when Capulet calls him back, proposes an early marriage date, and assures Paris that Juliet will be ruled by him. "I will make a desperate tender / Of my child's love," he says. And, "Do you like this haste?"

It's a 180 degree change by Juliet's father, as though with Tybalt gone, there was in the family's blood line some imperative that demanded that Old Capulet fill the vacuum left by his nephew's impetuous, hot temper. His reversal dooms any hope of a reciprocal bond with his only heir. He does, indeed, make "a desperate tender," and on the next morning, after the lovers' magical consummation night, both parents tell Juliet she is to marry the County Paris. Her objection is simple and rational: "What's the rush? I haven't even met him."

> I wonder at this haste, that I must wed
> Ere he that should be husband comes to woo.

Capulet loses his temper and calls Juliet a spoiled hussy, a "baggage," and a "tallow-face" full of "green-sickness carrion." His outburst shocks both his wife and the Nurse. Juliet responds with the ultimate Shakespearean gesture of loving respect: "Good father, I beseech you *on my knees*" (3.5.158, italics mine).[38] But Old Capulet is not to be gainsaid. He reverts to patriarchal type, telling Juliet she is his property to give away as he sees fit:

> And you be not, hang! Beg! Starve! Die in the streets!
> For by my soul I'll ne'er acknowledge thee,
> Nor what is mine shall never do thee good.

Echoes of Joan's father: "Dost thou deny thy father, cursed drab?/ Oh, burn her, burn her! Hanging is too good." Both fathers destroy the father-daughter bond

---

38. Cf., for example, Hamlet to Gertrude, "And when you are desirous to be blest,/ I'll blessing beg of you" (3.4.173-174), and Cordelia to Lear, "O look upon me, sir,/ And hold your hands in benediction o'er me!/ No, sir, you must not kneel" (4.7.57-59).

and pave the way for their daughters' deaths. Capulet's outburst means that both he and Juliet will "wither in their pride," one unto death and the other to his eternal grief. Juliet's appeal to "sweet my mother" falls on deaf ears: "Talk not to me, for I'll not speak a word./ Do as thou wilt, for I have done with thee." So her father disowns her, and both parents cast her away. Soon the Nurse will also turn her back, and later, so will Friar Laurence. All of Juliet's support falls away – except Romeo and Paris, and they can help her not.

The next time Capulet sees his daughter, she kneels again, but this time in mock obedience, speaking a false language, for Juliet knows what he will soon find out, that their bond of trust has been severed forever. And by the morrow, the words he speaks to her – that is, to her inert body -- are: "Death lies on her like an untimely frost/ Upon the sweetest flower of all the field" (4.5.28-29). How easily that compliment flows from his lips now, when obedience is no longer at issue. And now Old Capulet, despite his strong oath of 3.5, must "acknowledge thee" and see his daughter dead, not "in the streets" but in his own house, and he will have to bear the consequences forever.

By 1595-96, the pattern that Fiedler identified in *1 Henry VI,* of the daughter denying the father and subsequently dying, in *Romeo and Juliet* becomes more complex. Parental separation is a clear thread in Juliet's mind, for the famous balcony scene begins this way:

> O Romeo, Romeo, wherefore art thou Romeo?
> Deny thy father, and refuse thy name.
> Or if thou wilt not, be but sworn my love
> And I'll no longer be a Capulet.   (2.2.33-6)

In a gender reversal from Joan in *1 Henry VI,* Juliet urges Romeo to deny his father and then offers to deny hers in order to sweep away all external encumbrances to their love. It's a far cry from Joan's denial, part and parcel of the role she chose to play vis-à-vis both the French and the pursuing English. Juliet and Romeo *must* separate from their families because the Capulets and Montagues are trapped in an ancient, death-dealing feud. The lovers seek a new kind of life, one free from family and centered on their mutual love. But family encumbrances, like hoops of steel, are too strong, and their ecstatic love leads only to the tomb.

The cause of Juliet's death is not her refusal to obey her father. It is the sudden, volcanic ecstasy of meeting her soul mate in a city that is walled in with civil brawls, a city that produces a Mercutio and a Tybalt but which offers neither solace nor space for these young lovers. Such a city forces Romeo to woo Juliet unconventionally – in secret and in defiance of family tradition. Paris, on the other hand, plays by the book, wooing only Juliet's father. Indeed, the play demonstrates that in Verona, a walled city riven by an ancient family feud that the Prince seems powerless or perhaps unwilling to control, both conventional and unconventional love are doomed. In this environment, doomed also is any attempt by a daughter to create and nurture a bond of mutual love and trust with her father. About eight years later, Shakespeare took a stab at that pattern in *All's Well That Ends Well*,[39] and then assayed it again in three years with *King Lear.* Its full flowering

---

39. See footnote 4, on p. 9.

would have to wait until his last solo drama, about seventeen years after *Romeo and Juliet,* in *The Tempest.*

If Juliet was trapped in the *Grand-Guignol* of her family's grudge, where stood Romeo? In order to gain access to the Capulet's conservatory, he had to scale their garden wall, and enter, in Marjorie Garber's words, "the *hortus conclusus* (hidden garden), ... a traditional iconographic emblem of virginity in poetry and art (the Song of Songs, Chaucer's 'Knight's Tale,' the Unicorn tapestries)." Unbeknownst to him, the Capulet garden involved both "love and risk."[40] Although Romeo, unlike the poet of the sonnets, did not have to cope with a duplicitous Dark Lady, his cultural inheritance included the Petrarchan world of chivalry which will soon put at risk everything he thought he had just discovered about ecstatic love.

In confiding to the audience what is happening, the Chorus opens both Acts One and Two of *Romeo and Juliet* with sonnets. The "star-crossed lovers" celebrate their meeting with a shared sonnet (1.5.92-105),

---

40. Marjorie Garber, *Shakespeare After All*. Anchor (2004)199.

punctuated with their first kiss. Poet Glyn Maxwell wrote that "the shared sonnet conjures the miraculous element of *listening silence* – Romeo and Juliet during each other's lines ...."[41] Brian Gibbons artfully describes this kiss as "a perfect symbol of the absorption of the sonnet mode into the art of the play ...."[42] It's Petrarchan tradition absorbed into Elizabethan drama, a poetic mode brought to life by the two young lovers who are determined to scale the wall society imposes between them. It's also Shakespeare's retelling of Ovid's Pyramus and Thisbe, a story that sunk deeply into Shakespeare's imagination. In this most famous love story, Shakespeare shifts the focus just enough to juxtapose a Veronese father-daughter conflict with a lyrical retelling of Ovid's famous wall,[43] so wonderfully spoofed by Bottom and his cohorts in *A Midsummer Night's Dream.*

---

41. Glyn Maxwell, "Eternal Lines." *The NYT Book Review.* February 1, 2015, p.20.
42. Brian Gibbons, ed. *The Arden Shakespeare Romeo and Juliet.* London, Thomas Nelson (2006), 43.
43. In Ovid, both fathers objected to the budding romance of their young children.

The wall of Babylon, like Capulet's garden wall, represents all that the lovers wish to o'er leap. As Mercutio and Tybalt spar and curse each other in Act Three, Romeo does his best to remain in his new role, metaphorically transported beyond Verona's violent streets, and not slip back into the city's ancient quarrel, a remnant of the world of chivalry. Both Mercutio and Tybalt are hot-headed and thrive in the world of civil brawls. Romeo's best pleas fall on deaf ears, and Mercutio falls by Tybalt's foul sword-play. As he is dying, three times he utters his famous imprecation: "A plague o' both your houses,"[44] as though warning Romeo not to succumb to both houses's ancient curse. Even with Mercutio's death knawing at him, Romeo could have averted disaster had he not accepted the honor code's strict summons of revenge, of an eye for an eye, sounding much like Laertes, five years later. But he cannot resist viewing Tybalt's return to the public square

---

44. Mercutio's malediction would have resonated with Shakespeare's audiences. As Jonathan Bate reminds us, "Plague was the single most powerful force shaping his [Shakespeare's] life and those of his contemporaries." *Soul of the Age.* New York, Random House (2009), 4.

as a personal challenge: "Away to heaven respective lenity, / And fire-ey'd fury be my conduct now." How very different from his posture and his language at the opening of the balcony scene: "But soft, what light through yonder window breaks?/ It is the east and Juliet is the sun." Those two worlds are vastly different and cannot survive together; nor can Romeo bestride them both, like a Colossus. Immediately he kills Tybalt, he recognizes the utter gravity of his mistake: "O, I am fortune's fool" (3.1.138). His action, dictated by the chivalric honor code, adds fire to the ancient feud and leads directly to his separation from Juliet and the rapidly escalating, grim denouement of the drama.

Romeo's response to the dead body of Tybalt represents something very unusual in this play. He realizes that by acceding to his lust for revenge, by killing Juliet's cousin, he has, in one fell swoop, thrown away every chance he had to build a new and happy life with the girl of his dreams. His world goes from the promise of plus-ten to the certainty of minus-ten. It all happens in one instant. I cannot think of any other

Shakespeare tragedy where the end-game changes, radically changes, so quickly. King Lear learns how to become a man gradually, as he experiences the disdain of two of his daughters. Othello ingests Iago's poison bit by bit, not all at once. Macbeth succumbs to his hidden ambition day by day, as his wife and the witches go to work on killing his good instincts. Antony loses half the world in fits and starts, not all of a sudden. Hamlet is not able to revenge his father until the very end, and then only through the duplicity of Laertes and Claudius. There's no quick turnabout there either. Poor Romeo loses everything with the thrust of a sword blade. That's it. Ballgame's over. It is as though Shakespeare is telling us that it's always the kids who get hit hardest. Their vulnerability increases the tragic dimension.

But even before this critical turning point, in both their early meetings Juliet had instinctive forebodings. As all the guests are leaving Capulet's garden, in Act One, Juliet ponders her tête-à-tête and sudden kiss with a stranger. The Nurse tells her that the intruder is a Montague. "My only love sprung from my only hate"

(1.5.137) she sadly keens. Alone with Romeo that evening, just before they agree to marry:

> I have no joy of this contract tonight:
> It is too rash, too unadvis'd, too sudden,
> Too like the lightning, which doth cease to be
> Ere one can say 'It lightens.' (2.2.117-20)

And at their last meeting, before Romeo leaves for exile in Mantua:

> O think'st thou we shall ever meet again? ....
> O God, I have an ill-divining soul!
> Methinks I see thee, now thou art so low,
> As one dead in the bottom of a tomb.[45] (3.5.51-6)

One wonders what would have happened had Juliet acted on her instinctive fears. But another instinct, her profoundly felt love for Romeo, overpowered all her doubts. Acting on some deep, inner compulsion that led her to enfold her "only hate" with all her body and soul, Juliet forged ahead, trusting that somehow, someway, her ghostly father's "distilling liquor" would unite her

_____

45. Here we see Juliet prophesying, and only too accurately. Theoretically, then, Juliet qualifies as a witch, but she is too heavenly to bear that burden.

with Romeo, now ironically and actually beyond Verona's walls, banished to Mantua. Her one objective, as she told Friar Laurence, was "To live an unstain'd wife to my sweet love" (4.1.88).[46] But in *Romeo and Juliet* there was no resolute woman, as there will be in *The Winter's Tale,* who could act as an agent of regeneration and free the young lovers from the shackles of their parents and their walled society. Both Friar Laurence and Juliet's Nurse tried to do so, but all occasions did inform against the Veronese lovers, as they did against Pyramus and Thisby, the Babylonian pair. For Romeo and Juliet there was no lioness and no bloodied scarf, but their mulberry tree would also turn from white to deep purple, forever witnessing that No, Juliet never had a chance.

■ *A Midsummer Night's Dream*

> Be kind and courteous to this gentleman...
> Nod to him, elves, and do him courtesies.

---

46. Desdemona could have said exactly this. How sad that both young, innocent women die.

No lover in all of Shakespeare was more affectionately cosseted than Bottom in *A Midsummer Night's Dream*. And no rendezvous between seducer and seducee was so full of the music of good-hearted endearment as that between Titania and Bottom. There is no lust in Bottom's heart and probably none in Titania's. Although bedazzled by Puck's flower-juice, Titania recognizes Bottom as the real thing, in some respects more so than her mate, Oberon. So she instructs her fairy handmaidens to

> Be kind and courteous to this gentleman;
> Hop in his walks, and gambol in his eyes;
> Feed him with apricocks and dewberries,
> The honey bags steal from the humblebees ...
> To have my love to bed .... (3.1.165-72)

Bottom gets it right with the goddess: his love is woven of courtesy and warmth and benevolence and song. The four Athenian lovers in *A Midsummer Night's Dream* get it all wrong in this forest of escape until Puck undoes his innocent mistake and puts them to sleep in the bottom of the glen.

Composed at about the same time (1595-96) as *Romeo and Juliet, A Midsummer Night's Dream,* at first glance, can seem like *1 Henry VI* and *Romeo and Juliet* redux. The play opens with Theseus addressing the famous Amazon as "fair Hippolyta." Can this be that other well known *virago,* Joan of Arc, transported from France and tamed? And then, but nineteen lines later, who should enter but Old Capulet's counterpart, Egeus, "full of vexation... with complaint/ Against my child, my daughter Hermia." Both fathers have the same problem – their daughters, considered parental property, do not wish to marry the men they have chosen. Capulet threatens to throw Juliet out on the streets and disown her; by and large we believe him. Egeus goes even farther. He asks Theseus, ruler of Athens, to invoke Athens's "ancient privilege" and put Hermia to death if she continues to favor Lysander over Demetrius, her father's choice.

As she is mine, I may dispose of her,
Which shall be either to this gentleman [Demetrius]
Or to her death.... (1.1.42-4)

Although at first we may believe Egeus, and certainly do not doubt his sincerity – after all, he vents for twenty-three lines – as the play unfolds we begin to see him as what Northrop Frye calls the *"senex iratus or heavy father,"* one of the "humorous blocking characters of comedy [who] are nearly always imposters…."[47] By "imposter" Frye means a character who disrupts or tries to disrupt the natural desires of the young lovers, destined to be incorporated into the social order by and by. Significantly, Egeus is the only character who does not undergo some kind of metamorphosis. Egeus in Act One is the same as Egeus in Act Four, after which this *senex iratus* gets his just reward -- he disappears, where to we know not.

In *Midsummer*, Egeus asks Athens's ruler to invoke what Frye calls "some absurd, cruel, or irrational law"[48] that sparks the action of the comedy. We are confident Shakespeare won't allow matters to come to such a pass. If we had any doubts, we may note that Egeus

----

47. From Northrop Frye's "The Mythos of Spring: Comedy," in his *Anatomy of Criticism.* Princeton, PU Press (1990), 172,
48. Frye, 166.

shares the intentions of the fathers of Pyramus and Thisbe, soon to be delightfully mocked in the play-within-the-play the mechanicals stage to celebrate the wedding of Theseus and Hippolyta. How differently Shakespeare uses the Pyramus and Thisbe myth in *Midsummer* from *Romeo and Juliet,* where the entire plot line can be said to be Shakespeare's "modernizing" the Babylonian story to Verona, with special emphasis on walls, what they keep out and what in.

Of more importance, Egeus's brawl with his daughter is a reflection of Oberon's with his mate, Titania, over the changeling boy. Titania recognizes the importance of restoring harmony in the fairy world, the world of nature. For her, discord is a disaster, on both the micro and macro levels:

> But with thy brawls thou hast disturb'd our sport.
> Therefore the winds, piping to us in vain,
> As in revenge have suck'd up from the sea
> Contagious fogs....
> The ox hath therefore stretch'd his yoke in vain,
> The ploughman lost his sweat, and the green corn
> Hath rotted ere his youth attain'd a beard....
> The human mortals want their winter cheer:

No night is now with hymn or carol blest....
The seasons alter ...
　　　And the mazed world ...
Now knows not which is which.
And this same progeny of evils comes
From our debate, from our dissension,
We are their parents and original. (2.1.87-117)

It is an amazing speech by Titania, linking the worlds of

imagination, nature, and humanity. She, more than

Oberon, understands that their quarrel must be

mended. When it is, Egeus's becomes irrelevant and

disappears. What she implies is that pig-headed fathers

should learn from nature the unique gift of a daughter,

both prized for itself as well as for its potential of

creating new life, another generation.

　　　As though he were listening, although we can

never be sure, Oberon takes the initiative to win back

Titania. How? By another Puckish trick – more elixir. In

preparing his strategy, Oberon confers with his

messenger, Puck, and in twenty-seven beautiful lines

(2.1.148-185) recalls a time when he observed Cupid,

"all arm'd," take aim at "a fair vestal, throned by the west."[49] But the arrow misses,

> Yet mark'd I where the bolt of Cupid fell:
> It fell upon a little western flower,
> Before milk-white, now purple with love's wound:
> And maidens call it 'love-in-idleness.' (2.1.165-8)

It's an echo from Ovid's *Pyramus and Thisbe,* in which their strategy includes hiding "in the shade/ of a certain tree – a tree which was tall and heavily laden/ with snow-white berries, a mulberry...." When Pyramus, thinking his plan has led his beloved to certain death, plunges his sword into his side, "splashed by the blood, the fruit on the mulberry tree was dyed/ to a red-black colour; the roots were likewise sodden below/ and tinged the hanging berries with a purplish hue."[50] But in Oberon's fairy kingdom, even so dire an echo as this is itself metamorphosed, and the "juice" of that flower will

---

49. The "fair vestal" is Queen Elizabeth, and Bloom tells us that "one function of this fairy vision is to constitute Shakespeare's largest and most direct tribute to his monarch during her lifetime." Bloom's paragraph, on p. 159, is well worth reading.
50. Ovid. *Metamorphoses.* David Raeburn, tr. London, Penguin (2004), 4.88-90.

flow anew to create restorative action for both fairies and human beings.

We're not sure that Oberon really understands (as surely Shakespeare does) that by providing Titania a new love object whom she can "crown with flowers" and "make all her joy," her maternal and sexual needs will be so satisfied that that she can easily "unown" the changeling boy. It is difficult to know just why Oberon so desperately wants the boy. Is it merely pique? Or is it because Titania has not given him a son, and since this one is from India, his lineage will be like Oberon's? Perhaps in winning back Oberon, Titania has the better of the exchange, for she does not lament losing the boy but only the female companionship of his mother: "Full often hath she gossiped by my side…." The death of her close friend in childbirth mirrors the loss of Hermia's and Helena's intimacy, "all schooldays' friendships, childhood innocence," one of the perverse "side effects" of life in the forest, something Juliet, forever walled in in Verona, never experienced.

So here are two plays, written at about the same time, in which daughters disobey their fathers in the critical question of matrimony. Both Juliet and Hermia are determined young women, and both Capulet and Egeus are bull-headed fathers, *senexes irati.* But it is as though Shakespeare wrote one play with his left hand, the other with his right. *Midsummer* is a cakewalk, even though, like *Romeo and Juliet,* it is a play about ownership.

All of the major characters of *Romeo and Juliet* are real people; they are convincing and capture our attention and, frequently, our fear. *Midsummer* is very different. Is the changeling boy real? We never see him on stage. He represents Oberon and Titania's argument over ownership, mirroring Egeus's claim to own his daughter, mirroring Theseus's claim that he has now "won" Hippolyta, mirroring the young male lovers' claims of ownership, which a little elixir dropped on their eyelids totally reverses, thus demonstrating that "the course of true love never did run smooth." Despite the happy ending, are we confident that Lysander owns

Hermia, that Demetrius (still drugged by play's end) owns Helena? Does it really matter which man gets which woman? Is there any "true love" in this play as there surely is in *Romeo and Juliet*?

As for Duke Theseus, we all know his history of female abandonment. He, too, is not a real character but only the means to demonstrate the power structure of society, to emasculate harsh Egeus, and to give form to Shakespeare's comic plot. His great moment comes in 5.1, instructing his once wild warrior wife that "the lunatic, the lover and the poet/ Are of imagination all compact." He says this to her privately, as it were, and as an introduction to the four lovers and six artisans. She responds with wonder:

> But all the story of the night told over,
> And all their minds transfigured so together,
> More witnesseth than fancy's images,
> And grows to something of great constancy;
> But, howsoever, strange and admirable. (5.1.23-7)

She must judge for herself whether any of these ten is the lunatic, the lover, or the poet, and if so, how that may affect her coming night of passion with the famous Duke. Hippolyta recognizes that their forest "sleep over" transfigured all four lovers, each of whom has now grown "constant," that is, true. In so doing, we know that Hippolyta is *sui generis* and not a new version of Joan, Shakespeare's early Amazon.

So, although Shakespeare is having fun with Theseus, Hippolyta, Hermia, Helena, Lysander, Demetrius, Oberon and Titania (and so are we), he has denied "reality" to all of them. Who's real in this romp of a play? Maybe Puck, that precursor of Ariel, if only because he recognizes "What fools these mortals be." But Puck's other name is Robin Goodfellow, and as Bloom points out, that was "once a popular name for the Devil."[51] But not to worry; Oberon, his strict mafia boss, won't allow him anything more than a few mischievous tricks.

Ah, but then there are the craftsmen, the lowest end of Athenian society, living very happily at the

---

51. Bloom, 151.

bottom of the social ladder. Each of them is a real person with a real job and with real emotions. The most real is Bottom the weaver, the only one who easily glides between all three social milieux – the court, the forest, and the marketplace. He is at home everywhere and, of course, is the only one, including Oberon, who sleeps with the goddess Titania and who can converse, oh so easily, with those delightful fairies Peaseblossom, Cobweb, Moth, and Mustardseed. Bravo, Bottom!

Peter Quince is also real, though not quite at Bottom's level (a delicious concept). Quince is putative Shakespeare, the creator and director of the play-within-the-play, poking fun at himself. A quince is a small tree that annually produces a golden yellow pear-like fruit and whose leaves are strongly perfumed. Did Shakespeare think he was odorous and could produce something golden only annually? And if so, was it *Romeo and Juliet* or *A Midsummer Night's Dream*?

And who owns Bottom, or, to put the question another way, does Bottom know himself? When he awakens, no longer enchanted by the goddess's entwining arms, he tries to analyze his recent halcyon experience. The best this most human character can say, in his most lyrical outpouring (4.1.208ff), is that "I have had a most rare vision. I have had a dream past the wit of man to say what dream it was…. It shall be called 'Bottom's Dream,' because it hath no bottom; and I will sing it in the latter end of a play, before the Duke. Peradventure to make it more gracious, I shall sing it at her death."[52] Twice he promises us a song. How typical of Bottom. How different from Adonis who used every trick he knew to avoid what Bottom so thoroughly enjoyed. Bottom is also Shakespeare, telling us, some fifteen years later, "We are such stuff/ As dreams are made on, and our little life/ Is rounded with a sleep."

Comedies should end, Frye tells us, with a "festive ritual," with a return to a "normal" society, though frequently different from and better than that of the

---

52. At whose death? We're not certain, but I'll go along with Wolfgang Clemens, editor of the Signet edition, who believes Bottom is referring to Thisbe's death. But it's conceivable Bottom is referring to Titania and thus personifying his woodland bedmate. In his *Midsummer* chapter, Bloom points out that ll. 214-217, beginning, "The eye of man hath not heard," is Bottom's "audacious" parody of 1 Corinthians 2:9.

opening, and with "some twist in the plot [that] enables the hero to have his will," presumably with the girl of his dreams.[53] In *Midsummer,* we have three weddings, all of them blessed by Oberon and Titania (former lovers of Hippolyta and Theseus) and by bard Bottom's off-Broadway buddies. Athens in Act Five assuredly *is* a better place than in Act One. First, because Duke Theseus not only "overbears" Egeus's will but then invites the two couples, now presumably correctly paired (because of Puck's elixir, the plot's "twist"), to be "eternally knit" in his palace, to view with him and his Queen a pageant, and to spend their evening of ecstasy under his eaves. And second, because the Duke chooses the masque (really an anti-masque) that Bottom and his friends have so laboriously prepared to celebrate the royal solemnities.

That leaves us with the question of identifying the hero. Not Oberon, because even though he's won the custody fight, he's not really human. Not the Duke, who's missing from the entire middle of the play.

---

53. See Frye, 163.

Neither Demetrius nor Lysander, for they are mirror images and almost Tweedle-Dum and Tweedle-Dee. My strong vote is for Bottom, "Shakespeare's Everyman,"[54] a lover of songs and of all peoples, the surrogate for Pyramus, though willing to play any part, and the only one in the play who actually has a dream, thus validating Shakespeare's' title. And who is the girl of his dreams, the lass with whom he had his way?[55] Need you ask? Why, the goddess Titania, of course.

So while in *Romeo and Juliet* Shakespeare could probe the devastating effects of a father and daughter locked in the steel embrace of a patriarchal society walled in by an ancient vendetta, in *Midsummer* Shakespeare unlocked the strictures and chuckled at the seriousness of all the characters at every level of society, some pretending they were important, others knowing they weren't. By the end of his early career,

---

54. Bloom's happy label.
55. "Had his way" is lighthearted poetic license, for Titania really seduced Bottom, who instinctively knew how not to resist a comely goddess.

Shakespeare was at ease working within the Elizabethan conventions of his day as well as blowing them apart. Must the disobeying daughter pay a high price? Well, only sometimes.

■ The Merchant of Venice

> The quality of mercy is not strained.
> It droppeth as the gentle rain from heaven
> Upon the place beneath. It is twice blest:
> It blesseth him that gives and him that takes.
> 'Tis mightiest in the mightiest; it becomes
> The thronèd monarch better than his crown. ...
> But mercy is above this sceptered sway.
> It is enthronèd in the hearts of kings;
> It is an attribute to God Himself....

Within a year, Shakespeare was back at his writing desk examining with a scalpel both the father-daughter relationship and the impact on talented individuals of a society that could not understand two men whose lives and livelihoods stood beyond the pale. In the space of about two years, 1595-1597, Shakespeare wrote a heart rending tragedy, a frolic of a comedy, and then *The Merchant of Venice,* a play that really defies definition.

True, it ends in three marriages and no one dies, but is it really a comedy? More than forty years ago, Graham Midgley wrote that "seen from any angle, *The Merchant of Venice* is not a very funny play." He called it "a twin study in loneliness," the "twins" being Shylock and Antonio.[56]

The Merchant of Venice explores and stages three legacies: 1) Christian mercy vs. Jewish justice; 2) Jewish mercantilism in tension with its Christian host and ruler; and 3) heterosexual vs. homosexual love. Within this non-comedy are two very different daughter-father relationships. One of these daughters, Portia, is the linchpin of the plot, but since Shylock and Antonio are the key players, the "twins," we should first look at them, bearing in mind that all three are outsiders. Portia lives not in Venice but on a nearby island sanctuary. Because he is Jewish, Shylock is alien to Venice's Christian society and is treated as such.[57] Antonio, whose first speech opens the play --"In sooth I know not

56. Graham Midgley. "*The Merchant of Venice*: A Reconsideration." *Essays in Criticism 10* (April, 1960), 121.
57. Midgley says, "Shylock is treated as dirt," 123.

why I am so sad" – is not only sad but also lonely. He is a stranger to all the heterosexual romances of the play, a holdover from the poet's friend in the sonnets and a precursor to those two solo players, Hamlet and Horatio.

Early in the play, the twins' relationship is summarized by Shylock when he says, "He [Antonio] hates our sacred nation…. Cursed be my tribe/ If I forgive him" (1.3.38-42)! We should not be surprised. Forgiveness, a Christian "virtue," is alien to Shylock. Presented as polar opposites and as enemies, the Jew and the Christian are both men of commerce, who venture their substance in search of profit, and recognize and value Venice's commitment to uphold commercial contracts as key to "the justice of the state" (3.3.29). This contract with the state is a "bond" that Venice imposes on Shylock and Antonio alike and which they, in turn, hold reciprocally with Venice. Hence, Shylock does not exaggerate the importance of his personal bond with Antonio which Antonio fully and freely acknowledges. In addition, Antonio is bound to his friend Bassanio, much as Shylock is bound to his daughter, his religion, and his diamonds.

After Bassanio broaches the loan idea and Shylock meets Antonio, the Jewish banker, clearly interested, first airs his grievance against Antonio:

> Signor Antonio, many a time and oft
> In the Rialto you have rated me
> About my moneys and my usances. ...
> You call me misbeliever, cut-throat dog,
> And spit upon my Jewish gabardine,
> And all for use of that which is mine own.
>
> (1.3.102-9)

Can we blame Shylock for viewing Antonio with suspicion and hostility? Yet shortly thereafter, when Shylock and Antonio negotiate, Shylock steps across a centuries-old gap and offers to make an interest-free loan to this man who called him a cut-throat dog and spat upon him.

> I would be friends with you and have your love,
> Forget the shames that you have stained me with,
> Supply your present wants and take no doit
> Of usance for my moneys.... (1.3.134-7)

The dialogue between Christian and Jew sparkles with a love-hate patina, looking very much as though each side is doing his best to bridge the gap. For his part, Antonio's advice that Shylock view the loan not to a friend but "to thine enemy,/ Who if he break, thou mayest with better face/ Exact the penalty" (1.3.130-132), provides a clear opening for Shylock to tell Antonio that the default price of a pound of flesh simply gives the transaction the look of "sport." It is almost as though Antonio planted the idea with Shylock.

Then what prevents Shylock's extraordinary gesture to waive interest from ripening into some kind of friendship? The play's only living father-daughter relationship goes badly awry. Behind Shylock's back, his daughter Jessica was engaging in a different transaction. She had fallen in love with the Christian Lorenzo, who promised that they could elope and she could forever leave her father's house, which she calls "hell." Bad enough, but the elopement occurs at the very moment Shylock is dining with Bassanio and his Christian buddies, despite having told Bassanio, "I will buy with you, sell with you, talk with you, walk with you and so following. But I will not eat with you, drink with you nor pray with you." (1.3.31-34) When Shylock returns home, not only is Jessica missing, so also is a casket of diamonds and the very ring Shylock's wife Leah had given him as an engagement gift. Shylock's beneficence turns bitter, like a love song transposed to a minor key.

When Shylock agrees to the loan and sets the price of the bond's default at a pound of flesh "to be cut off and taken / In what part of your body pleaseth me" (1.3.141-142), he immediately raises the spectre of circumcision, one of the reasons one man comes at another with a knife. Will Shylock try to convert Antonio to Judaism? Then they will be like tribal brothers, undoing the hostility each expressed in 1.3. At the end of the trial scene, Antonio, as part of his "mercy," demands that Shylock become a Christian. Antonio uses not a knife but a weapon equally sharp – Shylock's money. Tit for tat, measure for measure, and just as Antonio had predicted, "The Hebrew will turn Christian..." (1.3.170). Does that mean the two, finally, are one or, at the least, "twins"? Always astute Janet Adelman reads Shylock's "enforced conversion to Christianity ... [as] in a sense a reenactment of that moment in human history when God's grace redeemed man from His Justice; it is achieved through the fulfillment of the law, as Christ promised."[58] Adelman underlines the paradox of Shylock's insistence that Venice's contract law be precisely fulfilled, and we should note that Shylock responds to Gratiano's harangue with, "I stand here for law" (4.1.142).

Throughout the play, Shylock and Antonio remain enemies. They converge through interesting Shakespearean back alleys, so much so that Portia, despite her wisdom, as she enters the courtroom must inquire, "Which is the merchant here, and which the Jew?" (4.1.169). And lest my gentle reader think that talk of circumcision is too far afield, we are reminded of Shylock's two references to Abraham (1.3.63, 152) along

---

58. Janet Adelman. *The Common Liar*. New Haven, Yale (1973), 5.

with other Biblical allusions. In the akedah scene[59], on Mount Moriah, Abraham almost takes a knife to his son, Isaac, which leads us to Jacob, mentioned eight times in Act I, Scene 3, alone. And from Jacob we go to Leah, one of Jacob's wives and, most importantly, the name of Shylock's wife. And we are reminded that Leah became Jacob's wife through deception. He thought he was marrying Rachel, his favorite, but at the last minute Laban, the girls's father, substituted Leah, just as Jacob, through deception, stole his twin brother's birthright. So many years ago, Laban established the pattern of a deceitful father who treats daughters like property.

In *The Merchant of Venice,* Shylock is plagued by deception, first by his daughter, Jessica, and then by his *hubris* when he thinks Venetian Law will allow him to exact the term of his bond with Antonio. Is Shakespeare telling us that Shylock is Jacob writ new and that Venetian contract is akin to Old Testament covenant? And what about Portia's unnamed dead father? Is he

---

59. *Akedah* is the Hebrew word for Isaac's terrifying experience on Mount Moriah, translated by Bloom as "intended sacrifice." See Genesis 22.

another Laban, reaching beyond the grave to control his daughter's choice of husband by his clever three-casket trial, whose key feature cleverly deceives?

Despite being walled in by the terms of her father's will, Portia acts with verve, humor, and intelligence. She clearly dominates every scene in which she appears. She saves Antonio, redeems the state's honor,[60] vanquishes Shylock, just as she vanquishes Morocco and Aragon, and outsmarts all the men. Unlike Jessica, Portia obeys her father and keeps the letter of his lottery law, though she is sorely tempted to bend the rules to give advantage to Bassanio. She lives in "Belmont," that is, on a "beautiful mountain or hill."

In the trial's opening scene, the Duke sets the stage by telling Antonio:

> I am sorry for thee. Thou art come to answer
> A stony adversary, an inhuman wretch,
> Uncapable of pity, void and empty
> From any dram of mercy. (4.1.3-6)

---

60. See the trial scene when the Duke almost dismisses the proceedings because Shylock has raised thorny questions about the universal application of Venetian law: 4.1.104-107.

It is as though for Shylock, the streets of Venice are made of quicksand. Antonio spat on him, and now the Duke, representing Venice's highest authority – the state itself – brands him "an inhuman wretch … void … of mercy." In some other play, Shakespeare would have created someone to offer Shylock a path to redemption. In this play, that someone could have been his daughter, Jessica, but she has already jumped ship, so we know Shylock's path leads straight downhill. Turning to Shylock, the Duke continues, "'tis thought,/ Thou'lt show thy mercy and remorse more strange/ Than is thy strange apparent cruelty…" (ll. 20-22). After reviewing the basic case facts, Portia also says to Shylock, "Then must the Jew be merciful" (l. 186). And then in her twenty-two line affirmation the learned young doctor from Rome, who actually lives on a beautiful mountain, famously tries to tell Shylock, and the court, how mankind should behave, one toward the other. It is her Sermon on the Mount. Her message echoes one of the beatitudes: "Blessed are the merciful, for they shall receive mercy." The audience knows this New

Testament message will fall deaf on Shylock's Old Testament ears,[61] even though he is scholarly enough to reply (scornfully) with a New Testament allusion to the scene of Jesus's crucifixion (Matt 27:25): "My deeds upon my head" (4.1.201). Or, continuing the Biblical metaphor, is Portia an echo of Eve, the naked woman who dresses and acts like a man to bring mercy or knowledge to mankind?

Portia is clearly the heroine of the story. What, then, are we to make of Jessica, the other daughter? Portia obeys her father's wishes. Jessica, on the other hand, is a five-star father-denier. She abandons his household, steals his substance, including the ring Leah had given him, abjures his religion, and marries Lorenzo, a Christian. Is there any punishment harsh enough for such perfidy?

---

61. We might add a minor footnote about Portia's advice "That in the course of justice none of us/ Should see salvation" (ll. 194-195). Personal salvation is not a concept in Judaism, only tribal or national salvation. It's one reason why Christianity was so appealing to many Jews (and Romans).

Perhaps there might be in *The Merchant of Venice, Part Two,* the (unwritten) sequel that follows Shylock after he leaves the courtroom, but not in the play as we have it. Shylock is such a villain that anyone abandoning his household is not only given a free pass but also wins kudos. Lancelot Gobbo leaves Shylock's employ and is transformed from a melancholy bit player to a joyful minor character who adds juice to several scenes. Lancelot's leaving, in 2.3, is our introduction to Jessica, who calls her father's abode "our house of hell," as though Shylock already has been consigned to a Christian punishment. Once alone, her thoughts turn to her *innamorato*:

> O Lorenzo,
> If thou keep promise, I shall end this strife,
> Become a Christian and thy loving wife.(2.3.19-21)

Within about two years of composing *Romeo and Juliet,* Shakespeare again treats us to a balcony scene where two lovers, from alien houses and under cover of darkness, pledge themselves to each other. Jessica is "above," looking out of a window in her father's house.

Lorenzo is "down" in the street below. In Verona, the lovers meet "by yonder blessed moon"; in Venice, Lorenzo exults that Jessica "must be my torchbearer" for the after-dark street masque that Lorenzo enjoys with his buddies, though you and I may wonder who is leading whom. And just as Juliet, though overjoyed, expressed forebodings (see pages 36-7, above), so Jessica thought it a "heinous sin ... / To be ashamed to be my father's child" and was "much ashamed of my exchange" [i.e., dressed as a boy and about to become a Christian]. Jessica and Lorenzo's language is not so suffused with poetry as is Romeo and Juliet's, yet the Venetian couple will find a kind of happiness while the Veronese two find only union in the tomb.

It is not, however, to Lancelot that we should compare Jessica, but to Portia, the other daughter. They are both prisoners of their fathers, both fathers would allow their daughters to be sacrificed,[62] both daughters play fast and loose with rings, both possess keys (Jessica

_____

62. Portia's to be sacrificed to "chance," Jessica, to a barren life in her father's evil, music-less household.

to her father's house, Portia to her father's caskets), both dress in men's clothes at critical moments, both express genuine love for the men they will marry, both know how to use caskets to secure their chosen lovers,[63] and both importantly relate to Bassanio and to Antonio.[64]

With all this going for her, does Jessica face any death threat? Is she Shakespeare's Venetian Joan of Arc or star-crossed Juliet? Actually she does, but only from her crazed father (in 3.1) discussing with Tubal his financial losses. In a kind of foretaste of Lear's mad banishment of Cordelia, Shylock vents, "I would my

---

63. Act 2, Scene 7, is devoted to the famous three caskets test, the outcome of which will determine who wins Portia. In the prior scene, the "balcony scene," Jessica gathers a cache of her father's money and jewels and tosses them to Lorenzo saying, "Here, catch this casket; it is worth the pains" (2.6.34).

64. Portia's ties to Bassanio and Antonio are obvious; Jessica's less so. As she and Lorenzo conclude their "balcony scene," they leave to attend Bassanio's masque feast. And immediately they leave, Antonio arrives to announce Bassanio's voyage to Belmont which will include Jessica and Lorenzo (though in a separate gondola to evade Shylock's search). See 2.6.48ff. And since Antonio in 1.3 has predicted, "The Hebrew will turn Christian," perhaps he has arrived to bless Jessica's apostasy as she sails off to Belmont with her gentle (and gentile) fiancé. See also 3.1, the antiphonal conversation between Shylock and Tubal: the bad news about Jessica's departure (Shylock's loss) vis-à-vis the good news about Antonio's shipping losses.

daughter were dead at my foot and the jewels in her ear; would she were hearsed at my foot and the ducats in her coffin." While we can understand his angry outburst, we know Jessica is safe since Shylock is the villain who will fail. The only other danger Jessica faces is metaphoric and beautifully staged. As the last act opens, the two *gentle* lovers, once again in the moonlight but now in Belmont, engage in a fond, rhetorical repartee ("On such a night as this") about famous but doomed lovers – Troilus and Cressida, Pyramus and Thisbe, Dido and Aeneas, and – are we surprised? -- Jessica and Lorenzo. It's a happy scene, prelude to an even happier one, with the only jarring note Jessica's admission that, like her father, she doesn't like music: "I am never merry when I hear sweet music" (5.1.77). It's probably inherited!

But Jessica's *coup de theatre* takes place two acts earlier. As Portia and Nerissa are about to leave Belmont, secretly to defend Antonio in court, Portia places the young couple in charge of her high hill, the locus of all virtue, beauty, friendship and love. She tells Lorenzo

> My people do already know my mind
> And will acknowledge you and Jessica
> In place of Lord Bassanio and myself. (3.4.38-40)

And, just in case we doubt that Jessica is worthy of such trust, in the very next scene Lorenzo asks her what she thinks of Portia. Her response is unequivocal: "Past all expressing … for the poor rude world / Hath not her fellow." So the merging of Jessica with Portia is complete, crowned with the news, fifteen lines from the play's ending, that Jessica will inherit Shylock's wealth.

Despite the concurrence of their first name's initial letters, Jessica is spared Joan's and Juliet's fates. Why? It is as though Shakespeare decided that her religious apostasy excused her from any patrilineal punishment. She chooses to live with Lorenzo in a Christian society, and even though she deserts her father with as much gusto as Joan, the playwright will punish her father instead of her. He is, after all, the villain of the piece. And, as noted above, Jessica's essence has merged with Portia's, the drama's heroine, so therefore she has earned immunity.

There remain then only two questions. The first regards Antonio. As the play nears its happy conclusion – happy for the lovers, that is – Bassanio invites Antonio to join him and Portia in Belmont for the night of the lovers' consummation. And Portia not only seconds the motion, but delivers the good news about his restored fortune:

> Antonio, you are welcome,
> And I have better news in store for you
> Than you expect. Unseal this letter soon.
> There you shall find three of your argosies
> Are richly come to harbor suddenly. (5.1.292-6)

So what is that all about? Is Antonio a kind of benign Pandarus, helping his dear friend Bassanio win and then re-win Portia? Or is he a surrogate for Portia's dead father, his three argosies akin to the three caskets that determined who Portia's husband would be? If so, in a real sense Antonio escorts Portia down the aisle to marry his friend Bassanio. And Antonio does the same for Jessica, standing in for his "twin," Shylock, who never would be allowed to set foot in Belmont where Jessica already has given one of his caskets to Lorenzo. Or perhaps the three argosies are Bassanio-Portia, Lorenzo-Jessica, and Gratiano-Nerissa, since Antonio played a role in each marriage. Perhaps Portia is astute enough to recognize that the loss of Antonio's ships is akin to his loss of Bassanio, and since the one has been found, why not restore the other.[65] Or is Antonio Adam to Portia's Eve and she is hinting that Bassanio is not quite man enough for her? After all, perhaps it was Antonio's privates that weighed a pound, and having saved him, she now wants her reward, her pound of flesh. Or is she slyly setting the stage for a Belmontian *ménage a trois*?

Probably not. My guess is that Shakespeare is up to his old game of "it's neither this nor that but a little of each," and the heterosexual and homosexual loves in the play cast disturbing shadows on each other, leaving neither pure or simple. This conundrum echoes the

---

65. See Marilyn French, *Shakespeare's Division of Experience*. New York, Summit Books (1981), 100-106.

poet's disturbing personal predicament, expressed (perhaps so many years ago) in the sonnets. The young poet preferred the love of his dependable male friend, with whom he could exchange intimacies, intellectual or otherwise. But along came the Dark Lady whose sexual attraction, Circe-like, was so powerful the poet could not resist. It was all well and good for the poet to upbraid himself for giving in, but what was he to do when the Dark Lady also seduced his friend, as in sonnet 133? Does he warn his friend not to fall into the trap he labels "hell?"[66] Does he berate himself for being jealous and then simply versify his quagmire, as in sonnet 144: "Two loves I have, of comfort and despair...."? Or does he try to find some way out of the labyrinth of triple jeopardy by creating Antonio of Venice?

If so, what really happens to Antonio in the play? He is both an insider, a rich member of Venice's elite, and an outsider, not part of any romantic couple seeking

---

66. As in sonnet 144: "To win me soon to hell my female evil / Tempteth my better angel from my side...."

a happy marriage. When Portia reveals that his ocean-bound gambles have paid off, his response is telling:

> Sweet lady, you have given me life and living;
> For here [in the letter she gave him] I read for certain
>   that my ships
> Are safely come to road. (5.1.306-8)

It echoes Shylock's, his "twin's" reaction to the Duke's sentence that spared his life and gave half his wealth to Antonio:

> Nay, take my life and all. Pardon not that.
> You take my house when you do take the prop
> That doth sustain my house; you take my life
> When you do take the means whereby I live.
>   (4.1.390-3)

So Portia has given Antonio "life and living" but not the one thing he most desires – happiness –which, as a woman, she can't provide. Like Jacques and Malvolio (and also Shylock), Antonio is the solitary man, a kind of Elizabethan melancholic without Hamlet's impulsive bent to strike first and ask questions later. Antonio is sad throughout the entire play while all those around him are pairing up, two by two, heading for the ark of love and happiness.

Indeed, Portia in the famous trial scene has defeated both "twins." Shylock's defeat is obvious, in fact, a drubbing. Antonio's is not so discernible. The Christian merchant believes his death is imminent, and has come to accept it. He only wishes to see Bassanio before he dies: "Pray God [he says to Solanio] Bassanio come / To see me pay his debt, and then I care not" (3.3.35-36), meaning "care not if I die." Of course, Bassanio reaches the courtroom, where the two friends enact a prequel to Hamlet's *adieu* to Horatio:

> You cannot be better employ'd, Bassanio,
> Than to live still and write mine epitaph.
>
> (4.1.117-8)

At this point, Antonio is seeking his own very lonely personal and spiritual victory, reflecting Christ as he speaks to his disciples, whom he tellingly calls "my friends," at the conclusion of the Last Supper: "This is my commandment, that ye love one another, as I have loved you. Greater love than this hath no man, when any man bestoweth his life for his friends" (John 15:12-13).

Antonio longs to give his life for his friend, and thus conquer death, Shylock, and the world. It would be a signal victory. His farewell to Bassanio is touching:

> Give me your hand, Bassanio, fare you well,
> Grieve not that I am fall'n to this for you:
> For herein Fortune shows herself more kind
> Than is her custom....
> Commend me to your honourable wife,
> Tell her the process of Antonio's end,
> Say how I loved you, speak me fair in death:
> And when the tale is told, bid her be the judge
> Whether Bassanio had not once a love....
> (4.1.261-73)

Antonio movingly describes his love for Bassanio: "bid her be the judge/ Whether Bassanio had not once a love….." But Portia's courtroom brilliance moves not in that direction. In effect, she denies Antonio his victory, and now we know why Antonio appears in Act Five. Defeated by not being able to bestow his life for Bassanio, he is a kind of ghostly spiritual father to all the lovers, one of whom is *his* love, far from his home in

Venice atop the beautiful mountain which was the site of Christ's Sermon on the Mount. As the conclusion of the play is enacted on stage, all the lovers slowly depart, two by two, leaving Antonio alone. His reply to Gratiano, so early in the play, is perfectly accurate at the end:

> I hold the world but as the world, Gratiano,
> A stage, where every man must play a part,
> And mine a sad one. (1.1.77-79)

Should Shakespeare have called the play *The Tragedy of the Merchant of Venice?* And what about Portia, whom we have called the play's "linchpin"? She obeys her dead father, dominates the action and thinking, and, like Rosalind two or three years later in *As You Like It,* wins her lover and teaches him how to be a true mate. So the pattern of father-daughter relationships remains important to Shakespeare, but in *Merchant,* a serious play, it becomes even more complex than in *Romeo and Juliet.* To begin with, we have two daughters, one of whose fathers is the villain, the other's dead before the play opens. Now, perhaps at most three years after *Romeo and Juliet,* Shakespeare decides for daughters.

The lesser of the two "saves" herself by making "correct" choices. The greater, obviously the play's heroine, faces every situation with brilliance, calm assurance, and clear insight into how an emotionally mature woman can find and win her happy husband, whether or not her father dictated the choice.

So can we then declare Portia victorious, winning out over whatever anti-feminine prejudices remain buried in her creator's mind? Perhaps -- except that we must recall that to win her twin courtroom victories in the play's central and most dramatic episode Portia had to dress like a man, calling herself Balthazar, the name of one of the three Wise Men who, following a star, came to pay homage to Mary and the Christ child.[67]

---

67. In her very thorough and knowledgeable article on the biblical sources for *The Merchant of Venice,* Barbara Lewalski provides a fuller gloss for Balthazar. Shylock's exclamation, when he thought he was winning, alluded to Daniel, "A Daniel come to judgment," from the apocryphal Book of Susanna. Lewalski points out that Daniel, in Hebrew, means "The Judgment of God," but in the Book of Daniel, his name is Baltassar, and the Book of Daniel foreshadows Christian tradition by "his humble appeal for mercy." See Barbara Lewalski. "Biblical Allusion and Allegory in *The Merchant of Venice." Shakespeare Quarterly* 13.3 (Summer, 1962): 327-343. The Balthazar quotation is from p. 340.

CHAPTER III. Women in Wartime
Troilus and Cressida, Antony and Cleopatra

■ *Troilus and Cressida*

> Words, words, mere words, no matter from the heart;
> Th'effect doth operate another way....
> My love with words and errors still she feeds,
> But edifies another with her deeds.

About a year before *Troilus and Cressida* was written, a legendary prince came reading:

> Gertrude: But look where sadly the poor wretch comes reading.
>
> Polonius: Away, I do beseech you both, away. I'll board him presently. (2.2.168-70)

It's the beginning of a famous scene in which Hamlet calls Polonius "a fishmonger" and tells the old man that he reads only "Words, words, words." In the last act of his mock epic, *Troilus and Cressida,* Shakespeare

---

68. With apologies to Jerome Kern.

caricatures his own earlier "word scene" when Pandarus, a Polonius who doesn't get killed, hands Troilus, another "poor wretch," a letter from Cressida, whom he had boarded only once. Hamlet derides his book because he knows Polonius wants to "board him," to know *his* contents, not the book's. Similarly, Troilus scoffs at the letter's contents because he believes Cressida has found contentment among the Greeks, and, to his sorrow, he has overheard Viola from concurrent *Twelfth Night* (perhaps playing next door), "They that dally nicely with words may quickly make them wanton" (3.1.14-15). So Troilus shreds her love letter, an apt symbol for what happens to every good intention or famous person in *Troilus and Cressida* – they all get shredded.

In this tableau scene, Troilus mocks his love affair amidst the most famous war of classical times – the struggle between Greeks and Trojans to avenge the theft of Helen. Shakespeare describes the warriors as "orgulous" (proud or haughty), a word he invented (sounding like "ogre") for this parody of a play, and which he never used again. Both the hero and the heroine degrade their love affair, and Cressida's relationship with her father is but a farce. Is this what a mere six years' passing did to the love affairs in *Romeo and Juliet* and *A Midsummer Night's Dream*, not to mention contemporary Orsino's plaintive pang, "If music be the food of love, play on"?

Nevertheless, the drama concerns two people desperately trying to find love and affection amidst difficult circumstances. One can wonder why, after so many fulsome love affairs, in city and in country, Shakespeare turned so negative. We have no answer, but perhaps Shakespeare dared to speculate about what would happen were he to transpose Romeo and Juliet into the Trojan camp, like some slight-of-hand circus magician.

Romeo and Juliet meet in Capulet's garden in Act 1, Scene 5. The words they exchange take the form of a sonnet, their exchange sealed with a kiss. It is pure romance (in the colloquial sense of that word). Troilus waits for Cressida also in a garden, but they do not meet until approximately midway through the play, in Act 3, scene 2. Romeo comes to Juliet directly, but Troilus says, "I cannot come to Cressid but by Pandar" (1.1.91), thus disparaging both himself, their rendezvous, and their future relationship. Juliet is probably wearing (or holding) a mask, appropriate to the evening's entertainment. Cressida meets Troilus veiled, as though she were not sure she wanted Troilus to see the real her, or as though she intuitively knew she should hold something back. How germane to the story that Pandarus, not Troilus, lifts her veil and that Pandarus urges the lovers to their first kiss.

Cressida's first words to Troilus are, "Will you walk in, my lord?", echoing Polonius's request to Hamlet (in 2.2), "Will you walk out of the air, my lord?" To which Hamlet responds, "Into my grave?" Is Cressida's invitation a trap for an unsuspecting and naïve Troilus? Is it a sexual invitation, or is the orchard of their tryst an Edenic Garden where Pandarus impersonates the tempting serpent, "more subtle than any beast of the field"[69], or is this orchard a killing field where

> Sleeping within my orchard,
>   ... thy uncle stole
> With juice of cursed hebenon in a vial,
> And in the porches of my ears did pour
> The leperous distilment.... (Hamlet, 1.5.59-64)

The orchard walls of *Romeo and Juliet,* which Romeo lept to come to his Juliet, are symbolic of the walls of Verona, where the family feud is too all-encompassing for the lovers to overcome. The feud in *Troilus and Cressida* is between two great and famous armies, met on the plains of Troy in "cruel war" to settle a grudge fight. And, like Montague vs. Capulet, Greek vs. Trojan will have a devastating impact on the lovers.

The parallels don't stop there. In the famous balcony scene, Juliet (rhetorically) urges Romeo to disavow his lineage:

> O Romeo, Romeo, wherefore art thou Romeo?
> Deny thy father, and refuse thy name.
> Or if thou wilt not, be but sworn my love

---

69. See Genesis 3:1.

And I'll no longer be a Capulet (2.2.33-6).

In 4.2, Pandarus tells Cressida that she is being exchanged for Antenor and therefore must return to her father, Calchas, who, having defected, is in the Grecian camp. She tries to refuse: "I will not go." When told she must, she, like Joan, denies her father:

> I will not, uncle. I have forgot my father
> I know no touch of consanguinity;
> No kin, no love, no blood, no soul so near me
> As the sweet Troilus. (4.2.97-100)

So once again we have a daughter who eschews her father, and we are led to wonder what punishment Shakespeare has in store. In *1 Henry VI,* Joan died, burned at the stake (though not on stage).

In a very real sense, Cressida's "punishment" lies at the heart of the overplot, to borrow Harry Levin's happy descriptive. After their night of arranged sex – for I cannot call it "love" – Troilus is ready to return to the world of men and leave Cressida to languish alone in bed. For her part, Cressida had hoped to find in Troilus someone who could bring her both sexual and emotional comfort, and her disappointment is real:

> Prithee, tarry. You men will never tarry.
> O foolish Cressid, I might have still held off,
> And then you would have tarried! (4.2.17-9)

Their farewell occupies the first 42 lines of Act 4, Scene 2, and includes Troilus's offhand observation that the lark ushers in a day that will be busy for him, when even the crows are "ribald." He speaks as though there is no *angst* in his heart at leaving Cressida:

> O Cressida! But that the busy day,
> Waked by the lark, hath roused the ribald crows,
> And dreaming night will hide our joys no longer,
> I would not from thee. (4.2.9-12)

The lovers share the scene with Pandarus, Cressida's uncle, her procurer, and the play's arch voyeur. Much more than Juliet's Nurse, the young lovers's sympathetic enabler, Pandarus relishes salacious comments. He enters with this cheerful greeting: "How now, how now, how go maidenheads?" To which Cressida is moved to retort, "Go hang yourself, you naughty mocking uncle!/ You bring me to do – and then you flout me too" (4.2.27-27). But for Cressida, there is also something naughtily delicious about her uncle's wicked wit, and in many scenes the two enjoy bantering with clever *double entendres.* In his Arden edition introduction, David Bevington writes that Pandarus's gloating humor is a thin disguise for his own incestuous feelings for his niece, making "for an uncomfortable moment in the theatre."[70] It's another echo between Pandarus and Polonius, as is Troilus's and Hamlet's mistrust of female sexuality and disappointment in woman's fidelity. Both protagonists could say, "Frailty, thy name is woman." These two plays, along with *Romeo and Juliet,* continue to talk to one another, *sotto voce.*

Romeo and Juliet's farewell scene is not much longer, the first 59 lines of Act 3, Scene 5, but the

---

70. David Bevington, ed. *The Arden Shakespeare Troilus and Cressida.* London, Thomson Learning (2006), 63.

contrast in tone, character, and lyrical quality could not be more vivid:

> Juliet: It is not yet near day.
> It was the nightingale and not the lark
> That pierc'd the fearful hollow of thine ear….
>
> Romeo: Look, love, what envious streaks
> Do lace the severing clouds in yonder east….
>
> Juliet: Yond light is not daylight, I know it, I.
> It is some meteor that the sun exhales
> To be to thee this night a torchbearer
> And light thee on thy way to Mantua.
>   (3.5.1-15)

Cressida's lines in 4.2 and 4.4, after learning that she must leave Troilus and return to her father in the Greek camp, reveal her at her best, her most poetic. In declaring her love for Troilus and her opposition to leaving the Trojan camp, she is at her zenith: "The grief is fine, full, perfect that I taste/…. How can I moderate it?/ … My love admits no qualifying dross;/ No more my grief, in such a precious loss" (4.4.3-10). To Cressida's beautifully sad "And is it true that I must go from Troy?", Troilus's sixteen line rejoinder is punctuated by sixteen negative words, like "rudely," "forcibly," and "injurious," with a passing reference, "so many thousand sighs," to Marlowe's famous line.[71] Troilus's speech captures the impact in tragedy of "Injurious Time." In this mock epic time allows the parting lovers but "a single famished kiss." Nine years later, Time will so transform *The Winter's Tale* protagonist that Leontes's kiss virtually imparts the breath of life into his seemingly spiritless wife.

But Troilus does seem to regret the loss of Cressida, a loss he knows, despite their mutual pledges, will be permanent. Like Romeo's, Troilus's predicament does not yield any solution. He lives in a world of men at war, and his first loyalty is to that struggle, not to an amorous struggle in Cressida's bed. In Chaucer's *Troilus and Criseyde* the lovers stay together for three full years. They develop a close relationship, and Criseyde, a very feminine woman of mystery and beauty, emerges as a precursor to Cleopatra. The great Egyptian Queen

---

71. "Was this the face that launch'd a thousand ships, / And burnt the topless towers of Ilium." Dr. Faustus, 5.1.87-8.

remains faithful to Antony by embracing an asp from Nilus's mud: "Dost thou not see my baby at my breast,/ That sucks the nurse asleep?" (5.2.309-310) Once in the Greek camp, Cressida, exchanged against her will, cannot remain faithful to Troilus. She must deal with her new reality as best she can.

In Shakespeare's sham epic, the lovers enjoy only one night together before all their troubles ensue. What Cressida had hoped for the poet had penned in Sonnet 116: "Love alters not with his brief hours and weeks,/ But bears it out even to the edge of doom." In this satire of a play, time is not on the lovers' side. To Cressida's "I must, then, to the Grecians?" Troilus can offer only, "No remedy," a response that reprises the theme of male ownership of women, inherited from *Romeo and Juliet,* *A Midsummer Nights' Dream,* and *The Merchant of Venice.* Although he later seeks Diomedes to get revenge on the battlefield, nothing is settled, just as nothing is settled between Menelaus and Paris. These two unchivalric battles over women symbolize the bogus epic and the satiric tone of this play. What is worse,

Troilus and Cressida ends with an even more satiric and horrific slaughter when Achilles, against all the rules of manhood and honor, orders his *Mafia* henchmen, the Myrmidons, to attack and kill unarmed Hector. And so the last battle scene of the play spotlights the great Achilles as a depraved coward instead of the fabled hero who, once he decides to fight, turns the tide against the Trojans in *The Iliad.*

Once on the Greek side, it is all downhill for Cressida. She is paraded before the lustful Greeks like a prostitute displayed to potential customers for the highest bodily bid. Ulysses, one of the ironic truth-sayers on the Greek side, refuses to play his fellows' game of begging Cressida for a kiss:

> Fie, fie upon her!
>   ... her wanton spirits look out
> At every joint and motive of her body....
>   Set them down
> For sluttish spoils of opportunity
> And daughters of the game. (4.5.55-64)

For Ulysses, "daughters of the game" expresses everything that is demeaning about this war over a stolen woman as well as the ferrying of both men and women across the supposedly fierce and heroic battle line. Fie upon it!

Paradoxically, Calchas, her own father, initiates the "prisoner exchange," Antenor for Cressida, and once again we see daughters as property, so devastatingly presented four years later in *King Lear.* Calchas's 28-line request to Agamemnon, in 3.3, is the only time we see him on stage, as though Shakespeare were saying, "He doesn't deserve any more face-time." We should not be surprised, since Calchas is bunking with Menelaus, whose cuckolding started the war. In his last appearance, offstage in 5.2, with just four words he turns his daughter over to the waiting Diomedes: "She comes to you" (5.2.5).[72] Joan of Arc's father, James, a "sorry shepherd," seeing her perilous plight, offered to die with his daughter. Calchas, not even a pale imitation of James, is another Pandarus, another Polonius, willing to use his daughter to serve his sordid political purpose.

---

72. In *The Iliad,* Calchas is a prophet who tells Agamemnon the cause of the fierce plague that is devastating the Greek army.

How fitting to the spirit of the play that Pandarus, the linchpin of Troilus and Cressida's assignation, enters the play at line 6 and is the last character we see on stage, bequeathing the audience (and that includes you and me) all his diseases. In the end, after all his plotting, his jibes, his dirty jokes, he walks alone, a solitary figure, like a debased Antonio of *The Merchant of Venice.* Polonius, on the other hand, after ruining his daughter's chances for happiness, is dispatched midway through *Hamlet,* his usefulness to the story exhausted and his *persona* negated: "I took thee for thy better."

After Troilus has abandoned her, and without the protection of her father, Cressida is left helpless to Diomedes's cold lust. Only her feminine wiles buttress her against personal disaster. In the last act of her story, we see her playing fast and loose with Troilus's sleeve, a memento that supposedly symbolized the lovers' devotion and loyalty to each other.[73] Like Othello and

---

73. Shakespeare was fond of such mementos, used to signify different things in different contexts. Cf. Juliet's ring in Romeo and Juliet, Portia's and Jessica's rings in *Merchant*, and the fatal handkerchief in *Othello*, all

Iago overhearing Cassio and Bianca, or Polonius's several eavesdroppings (which end fatally), Ulysses brings Troilus within earshot of Cressida and her Greek "patron." After the voyeur-superior Thersites observes Troilus and Ulysses watching Cressida amorously tease Diomedes, he offers this succinct distillation of the play: "Lechery, lechery, still wars and lechery; nothing else holds fashion" (5.3.201-202).

Why should we be surprised? In 31 wry lines, the Prologue opens the play by telling us that the cause of the war is not territory or resistance to a tyrant but just a stolen woman and that the outcome is inconsequential. The war is a gamble, a roll of the dice, and which of these "diminished epic heroes"[74] wins matters not a whit. When Paris asks Diomedes who "merits fair Helen most,/ Myself or Menelaus?," his reply cogently summarizes this most cynical of Shakespeare's dramas:

---

of them stepchildren of Thisbe's scarf, scarfed and soiled by the bloodthirsty lioness.

74. Janet Adelman's phrase in *The Common Liar.* New Haven, Yale (1973), 54.

Both alike....
Hear me, Paris:
For every false drop in her bawdy veins
A Grecian's life hath sunk; for every scruple
Of her contaminated carrion weight
A Trojan hath been slain. (4.1.57-74)

"Her contaminated carrion weight," what a line, and how far we've come from Marlowe's famous "Was this the face that launch'd a thousand ships/ And burnt the topless towers of Ilium?" The dignified conventions of love and war are denuded of dignity, and nothing good and noble can come from Troilus and Cressida's romance. Her literary legacy becomes the very reputation she most feared: "As false as Cressid."

Sonnet 127 introduces the Dark Lady. It begins:

In the old age, black was not counted fair,
Or, if it were, it bore not beauty's name;
But now is black beauty's successive heir....
Therefore my mistress' eyes are raven black.

In these latter sonnets, not only does the poet confess that the Dark Lady's sensuality has enslaved him, it also enslaves the poet's friend, the man whom earlier he had preferred above everything and everyone. So when he learns that the Dark Lady is neither chaste nor true, his verse agonizes about his impossible situation, from which he cannot escape:

> When my love swears that she is made of truth
> I do believe her though I know she lies....
> On both sides thus is simple truth suppressed....
> Therefore I lie with her and she with me,
> And in our faults by lies we flattered be.[75]
>
> (Son. 138)

In his splendid introduction to the Arden edition, David Bevington notes that in *"Troilus and Cressida* Shakespeare unveils the terrifying spectre that has menacingly threatened his earlier plays in the shape of a male nightmare: the woman who is in fact untrue to her vows as a lover. The Dark Lady and Cressida do betray and cheat their men."[76] About midway through his remarkable dramatic career, the Dark Lady still held Shakespeare in her grip of steel, as did the bewitching

---

75. The double entendres are much like Cressida and Pandarus's badinage.
76. Bevington, 57.

and mysterious father-daughter enigma, here mockingly reduced to four forlorn words, "She comes to you."

Postscript:

In the theatre, *Troilus and Cressida* has come to be known as "Shakespeare's pacifist play." In the 1960s, both Joseph Papp and John Barton included obvious allusions to Vietnam in their productions. More recently, the Sound Theatre Company of Seattle opened its version in March, 2008, timed to coincide with the fifth anniversary of the U.S. invasion of Iraq. The play took place in a hangar of a former Navy base. One of the two veterans in the cast was sworn into the Navy in this very hangar. "Volunteers from Veterans Against the War had been invited to attend, and stood by the concessions before curtain and at intermission, manning tables smothered with leaflets denouncing President Bush's cowboy diplomacy. The presence of anti-war activists, the gumption of using a decommissioned military base to host a play that debunks military heroism, and the suspicion that Shakespeare's status as Our Ever-Hip

Contemporary was going to be reaffirmed yet again, all combined to generate an electric atmosphere." (From the University of Washington's Todd Borlik's review in *The Shakespeare Newsletter* Spring/Summer, 2008.)

■ *Antony and Cleopatra*

I dreamt there was an Emperor Antony.
O, such another sleep, that I might see
But such another man.

Is Cressida another incarnation of the Dark Lady, as Joan of Arc was? Is Cressida "dark?" In fact, do we know what Cressida looks like? Is she tall or short, blonde or brunette, thin or *zaftig*? Typically, nowhere does Shakespeare tell us. So, has Shakespeare --- finally, you might say – put the Dark Lady behind him?

Well, no. Within the first six lines of *Antony and Cleopatra,* written about five years after *Troilus and Cressida,* Philo complains to his fellow soldier, Demetrius, that their general now bends his warrior's eyes "Upon a tawny front." And to be sure we understand that these hardy foot soldiers are unhappy with Antony's infatuation with the tawny Queen of

Egypt, Philo complains that Antony's

> captain's heart ...
> Is become the bellows and the fan
> To cool a gypsy's lust.
> Take but good note, and you shall see in him
> The triple pillar of the world transformed
> Into a strumpet's fool.   (1.1.6-13)

In the first thirteen lines, Shakespeare highlights the

play's political though not central conflict.

    In Cleopatra do we once again have the Dark Lady

brought before us, again on stage, in full view? Is

Cleopatra a deceiver? Yes. A two-timer? Yes. Unreliable?

Yes. Untrue to her vows? Yes. A *femme fatale superieur?*

Yes. Years later, twentieth century lyricist Johnny

Mercer wrote:

> A woman's a two face
> A worrisome thing
> Who'll leave ya t'sing
> The blues in the night.

Did he have Cleopatra in mind? Of course. Yet also in the

twentieth century, Shakespearean scholar Harold Bloom

wrote that Cleopatra "is astonishingly good-natured, with a generosity of spirit unmatched in all of Shakespeare."[77] So what kind of a Dark Lady is this generous Queen of the Nile, and does Shakespeare approve or denounce her?

Politically, *Antony and Cleopatra* continues the story of *Julius Caesar,* when, after the assassination, Antony and Octavius join to rout the conspirators. But just as Caesar's murder opened a Pandora's box of political demons that ensnared Brutus and Cassius, their conquerors were themselves ill fated and soon enough were battling. But this time the prize was the entire civilized world. According to Plutarch, Cleopatra probably met Antony in Rome when she was staying with Julius Caesar and was "young and ignorant of the world."[78] In 41 BCE, after the Battle of Philippi, Antony, in command of Rome's eastern provinces, summoned Cleopatra to meet him in Tarsus, ostensibly to complain

---

77. Harold Bloom. *Shakespeare: The Invention of the Human.* New York, Riverhead (1998), 549.
78. From Dryden's translation of Plutarch, *Life of Antony.* Source is Penelope.uchicago.edu, via Google.

about her rumored support of Cassius or perhaps to secure a base there for further Roman conquests in the Mediterranean. Indeed, Shakespeare describes this meeting in *Antony and Cleopatra*, with Enorbarbus's famous limning: "The barge she sat in, like a burnished throne,/ Burned on the water..." (2.2.197-198). By now, Cleopatra was no longer "young and ignorant of the world."

Historically, then, *Antony and Cleopatra* is a sequel to *Julius Caesar.* But there are no lovers in *Julius Caesar,* and inevitably we think of *Romeo and Juliet* and even, scurrilous though the thought may be, of *Troilus and Cressida.* All three dramas are about love, war, and death, and all three are centered on an amorous couple, yet how different. In *Romeo and Juliet* the war has dragged on for decades before the play begins the ancient family feud of Montague vs. Capulet, Verona's *Grand Guignol.* Although the war is local, hemmed in by Verona's walls, the feud is deadly enough; its victims include Mercutio, Tybalt, the County Paris, and, finally, the lovers themselves. In *Troilus and Cressida,* we enter war *in medias res*. It, too, is a real war, though one borrowed from Homer. Its chief victim, Hector, is the most honest and noble warrior on either side. His grisly death debases and derogates Achilles, his killer, and utterly robs the war of any dignity. War in *Antony and Cleopatra* is also very real, involving the entire world from Tiber to Nile. There are six deaths – Eros, Enobarbus, Iras, Charmian, and the lovers -- all, paradoxically, caused by love, not war.

There is no romantic poetry in Troilus and Cressida's arranged tryst. Romeo and Juliet's young love affair is full of poetry, some of it the poetry of courtly love, all of it lyric. And so is Antony and Cleopatra's more mature, wanton, tempestuous, off-again, on-again attempts to understand both each other and themselves. Without much forethought, both Antony and Cleopatra decide to give up the world to gain eternity. Troilus and Cressida's love affair runs smack into the grim wall of war and history.

Shakespeare began his grisly family tragedy with King Lear's demanding of his daughters, "Which of you shall we say doth love us most..." (1.1.53). Now, about one year later, with Shakespeare perhaps leery of the results of that command, Cleopatra asks a similar question, her first words in the drama. But they are tossed at Antony with a coquettish grin: "If it be love indeed, tell me how much." His response is exactly what Cordelia should have said, "There's beggary in the love that can be reckoned" (1.1.11-12).

The scene is dominated by affectionate and intelligent badinage. Just before he dismisses the messenger undoubtedly bringing some demand from his erstwhile partner in Rome, Antony, in an eight-line speech, stakes his claim and defines the uniqueness of this couple:

> Let Rome in Tiber melt, and the wide arch
> Of the ranged empire fall! Here is my space,
> Kingdoms are clay: our dungy earth alike
> Feeds beast as man. The nobleness of man
> Is to do thus [presumably embracing
>   Cleopatra]; when such a mutual pair
> And such a twain can do't, in which I bind,
> On pain of punishment, the world to weet
> We stand up peerless. (1.1.33-49)

Her rejoinder is typical of their verbal encounters: "Excellent falsehood!" It is, after all, a play whose first words are, "Nay, but...." Nevertheless, the couple does indeed "stand up peerless," Antony will indeed receive his punishment, and despite his claim on "my space," Antony's kingdom will indeed shrink and then fall.

Plutarch explains that Caesar's ships were built for battle, not for "pomp," as were Cleopatra's, and that Caesar outmaneuvered Antony, separating him from his land-based army. Shakespeare omits these details and shows us Antony refusing the advice of Enobarbus, Canidius, and an unnamed soldier, choosing to fight Octavius by sea. He gives his comrades no reason except "that he dares us to't" (3.7.29). Nor does Shakespeare explain why Cleopatra entered her sixty sails in the first place and then turned tail. We do know why Antony followed her; he is smitten. So, is this Egyptian Dark Lady very different from the Dark Lady of the sonnets, whose Circe-like attraction enslaved the poet? Cleopatra unmans Antony, especially of his renowned military

judgment and bravura. No longer would he be capable
of such feats as Caesar described:

> Thou didst drink
> The stale of horses and the gilded puddle
> Which beasts would cough at....
> And all this ...
> Was borne so like a soldier that thy cheek
> So much as lanked not. (1.4.61-71)

Antony's military impotence reaches unto the gods
themselves. In a beautiful and mysterious tableau
(sometimes cut by niggardly directors), Antony's soldiers
hear strange music "under the earth.... 'Tis the god
Hercules, whom Antony loved,/ Now leaves him"
(4.3.12-16). Antony himself confesses to Eros, "O, thy
vile lady!/ She has robbed me of my sword" (4.14.23-
24). As Philo tells us early on, "you shall see in him/ The
triple pillar of the world transformed..." (1.1.11-12).

But this Dark Lady *is very* different. *Sui generis,*
she lives and breathes in a sphere unlike any woman
Shakespeare has yet created for us. In terms of largeness
of spirit and what Barbara Everitt calls "enormous

abundance of life,"[79] only Falstaff compares, the Henriad's larger-than-life mentor to Prince Hal. But Cleopatra lives in a different sphere. Falstaff is ultimately bound by political considerations. Cleopatra makes herself untouchable, ultimately by committing suicide. The epic nature of Shakespeare's tale also means she has the license of a great queen -- to borrow Lear's phrase, "every inch a queen." She is the last of the Ptolemies to rule Egypt. To a great extent, *Antony and Cleopatra* is a drama that explores and even justifies the untouchable freedom of this remarkable woman.

In the sonnets, love and death frequently are sexually evocative, with "dying" referring to the sudden plunge after orgasm. But in *Antony and Cleopatra*, death becomes the inevitable consequence of the hyperbolic love of these two peerless lovers. Their immersion in each other is more than sexual; in a sense, at the end, they become each other, and the difference of gender melts away, like Rome in Tiber. Octavius discerns it right

---

79. From her Introduction to the Signet edition of *The Tragedy of Antony and Cleopatra*. New York: Penguin (1988), xxxi.

away and tells Lepidus that Antony "is not more manlike/ Than Cleopatra, nor the Queen of Ptolemy/ More womanly than he…" (1.4.5-7). When Antony is away in Rome and Cleopatra reminisces with Charmian, the tawny Queen of Egypt relishes recounting one of their trysts:

> Ere the ninth hour, I drunk him to his bed;
> Then put my tires and mantles on him, whilst
> I wore his sword Philippan.   (2.5.21-3)

And in her monument, when the end is near, Cleopatra requests the guard give entrance to the "rural fellow," in reality a messenger from the gods, for he carries the asps in his basket of figs. At this moment, Cleopatra sheds her womanhood for good as she becomes asexual, ephemeral, and eternal (and very different from Lady Macbeth who asks the spirit to "unsex" her):

> Let him come in….
> He brings me liberty.
> My resolution's placed, and I have nothing
> Of woman in me: now from head to foot
> I am marble-constant: now the fleeting moon
> No planet is of mine. (5.2.235-41)

For the first and only time, Cleopatra becomes "marble-constant" and does not change her mind. She has cast away her flirtatious game with Antony and intently focuses on meeting her "husband" in eternity, the afterlife.

Thinking Cleopatra dead, Antony begins their antiphonal threnody:

> I will o'ertake thee, Cleopatra, and
> Weep for my pardon. So it must be, for now
> All length is torture: since the torch is out....
> I come, my queen. Stay for me. (4.14.44-50)

Then Antony attempts suicide and bungles it, as he has so much else in Egypt. Once again, Shakespeare gives us a balcony scene, with Cleopatra "above" in her monument, and Antony "below." As his guards haul Antony up into Cleopatra's monument, the poetry and drama become intense. When Antony dies in her arms, *pieta-like,* she laments:

> Noblest of men, woo't die?
> Hast thou no care of me? Shall I abide
> In this dull world, which in thy absence is

No better than a sty? O, see, my women,
The crown o' th' earth doth melt. My lord!
O, withered is the garland of the war,
The soldier's pole is fallen: young boys and girls
Are level now with men. The odds is gone,
And there is nothing left remarkable
Beneath the visiting moon. (4.15.59-68)

Her encomium, so different from anything in *Troilus and Cressida,* engenders a flashback to about six years earlier, to Hamlet's "How weary, stale, flat, and unprofitable/ Seem to me all the uses of this world" (1.2.133-134)! Hamlet was alone then; she is not.

Walter Cohen, in his Norton Critical Edition Introduction, postulates that Cleopatra does not resolve on suicide until "she becomes certain that Caesar plans to lead her in a humiliating triumph in Rome."[80] Politically astute, she does indeed send a messenger to Caesar to discern his plan. Her plan is to avoid humiliation in Rome from "some squeaking Cleopatra" and instead join Antony in eternity so ironically "after the high Roman fashion." She does so in one of the great

---

80. *The Norton Shakespeare Tragedies.* New York, Norton (1997), 857.

speeches in all of Shakespeare. It is her *liebestod,* as glorious as any music Richard Wagner ever wrote:

> Give me my robe, put on my crown, I have
> Immortal longings in me. Now no more
> The juice of Egypt's grape shall moist this lip.
> Yare, yare, good Iras; quick: methinks I hear
> Antony call: I see him rouse himself
> To praise my noble act....
>   Husband, I come:
> Now to that name my courage prove my title!
> I am fire, and air; my other elements
> I give to baser life. (5.2.280-90)

In his famous soliloquy, Hamlet cavils at "what dreams may come/ When we have shuffled off this mortal coil,/ Must give us pause" (3.1.66-68). But Antony and Cleopatra entertain no such qualms. They seek reunion in death.

With the ending of this great love drama, Shakespeare was able to take his Dark Lady and push her to an extreme, beyond ordinary bounds, and in so doing, give her extraordinary poetry. No longer Joan of Arc, who, since she was French and fought for the French, was destined to be burned at the stake. No longer Juliet who, though not a dark lady and willing to do anything for Romeo, was hemmed in by an ancient family feud within Verona's suffocating walls. And no longer Cressida, also not dark and hardly chaste or loyal, but abandoned by her father and her uncle and left to the mercies of the shallow Greeks.

Even cold, calculating Caesar, when confronting the Egyptian bodies and knowing the girls had stymied his grand plan, paid fitting tribute to this extraordinary woman:

> ... she looks like sleep,
> As she would catch another Antony
> In her strong toil of grace. (5.2.345-7)

But it was Charmian, the tawny Queen's charming handmaiden, just before embracing the asp herself, who said it best:

> So, fare thee well.
> Now boast thee, death, in thy possession lies
> A lass unparalleled. (5.2.314-16)

It is unlikely we will ever see a Dark Lady like this one again.

CHAPTER IV. Women in the High Tragedies

Hamlet, Othello, King Lear, Macbeth

■ *Hamlet*

Sweets to the sweet. Farewell.
I hop'd thou shouldst have been my Hamlet's wife:
I thought thy bride-bed to have deck'd, sweet maid,
And not have strew'd thy grave.

There are three different worlds in *Hamlet.* Sometimes they intersect. That they never merge creates a dramatic tension that never leaves the stage. The first one, appearing after only 43 lines, is the world of dynastic succession. Old Hamlet's world features wars fought *mano a mano,* whose outcome could determine empires.[82] The first three references to the ghost, all by Horatio, declaim his battle puissance:

---

81. With apologies to Rodgers and Hart.
82, Out of sheer desperation, Antony (in Act Three) dares Caesar to single combat. Antony came from the ghost's chivalric world, but Caesar had long since left that world behind. His reply, in essence, was, "You gotta be kidding!"

What art thou that usurp'st this time of night,
Together with that fair and warlike form
In which the majesty of buried Denmark
Did sometimes march? (1.1.49-52)

Such was the very armour he had on
When th'ambitious Norway combated.
So frown'd he once, when in an angry parle
He smote the sledded Polacks on the ice.[83]

(1.1.63-6)

    ... our last King
Whose image even but now appear'd to us,
Was as you know by Fortinbras of Norway,
Thereto prick'd on by a most emulate pride,
Dar'd to the combat; in which our valiant Hamlet
(So this side of our known world esteem'd him)
Did slay this Fortinbras.... (1.1.83-89)

And to emphasize his purpose, the ghost comes back

dressed in mail, "Armed at point exactly, cap-á-pie....

Arm'd, my lord ... from head to foot."[84] Anticipating

Hamlet's mini-lecture to the players, the ghost wishes to

hold his military mirror before Hamlet so that his son

---

83. Does the line not evoke visions of a brawl on the Rockefeller Center skating rink?
84. From this we learn that there's a dressing room in Purgatory. When old Hamlet was poisoned in his orchard, he was not wearing mail.

will also become a man of action. In fact, the ghost is ready for combat and wants his son, as his surrogate, to go into battle right away and slay the enemy, his brother. Quite naturally (or should we say "unnaturally"), the ghost assumes his son is also of his world, which is what he means when he says to Hamlet, "I find thee apt" (1.5.31).

But the ghost is mistaken. Young Hamlet is not "apt," he belongs to the world of studies, of philosophy, of words, of soliloquies. As Polonius later tells us, "sometimes he [young Hamlet] walks four hours together/ Here in the lobby [reading]" (2.2.160-161). Hamlet's contemplative speech to Rosencrantz and Guildenstern -- "I have of late ... lost all my mirth...." (2.2.295ff) -- would be Greek to his father. "What a piece of work is a man"? The ghost's response would have been something like "Balderdash. Just get on with your revenge," which is why the ghost reappears, in Gertrude's chamber: "Do not forget. This visitation/ Is but to whet thy almost blunted purpose" (3.4.110-111). During this third and final appearance, unlike his first two, the ghost is visible only to Hamlet. He has no message for anyone else and wears "his habit as he liv'd,"[85] almost as though he wished to climb back into bed with his winsome wife. In addition, he is a Catholic ghost; he emerges from purgatory, a bourne outside Protestant theology. Yet Hamlet is a student at Luther's university. When he tells his fellow Wittenberg student, "There are more things in heaven and earth, Horatio,/ Than are dreamt of in your philosophy" (1.5.174-175), that does not include a purgatory preceptorial. [86] The Catholic vs. Protestant undertone, while not a major concern for this reader, adds another, though minor, element of tension to the play.

Intuitively, Hamlet recognizes the gulf between himself and his father and acknowledges that the ghost belongs to a different world. In an early conversation with Horatio, Hamlet recalls his father: "A was a man,

---

85. The First Quarto describes the ghost dressed "in his night gowns." See the Arden Edition,3.4.103 fn.

86. "By 1530 Luther came to denounce the whole notion of Purgatory...." From Stephen Greenblatt, *Hamlet in Purgatory*. Princeton: PU (2001), 34. See pp. 33-35 for Luther's struggle with this Catholic concept.

take him for all in all:/ *I shall not look upon his like again*" (1.2.187-188, italics mine). In Claudius's Denmark, there are no more men of chivalry, and no one to rival the dead king. The poor ghost does not get his wish until the end of the play when Hamlet, almost by accident,[87] kills Claudius, and Fortinbras orders "four captains [to]/ Bear Hamlet *like a soldier* to the stage …/ and for his passage,/ *The soldier's music and the rite of war*/ Speak loudly for him" (5.2.400-405, italics mine).[88]

The third world is Claudius's. He is a pretender to old Hamlet's throne, and his court represents degenerate dynasty.[89] Not without personal courage (demonstrated when Laertes threatens him), he can

---

87. As John Lahr points out, "Even after his mother sips from the poisoned chalice meant for him and collapses, Hamlet doesn't know where to look. 'Let the door be lock'd. Treachery! Seek it out!'" Only after the dying Laertes tells Hamlet that "the King's to blame … does Hamlet, at the cost of his own life, take the revenge he's been willing himself to wreak since Act 1." John Lahr, *The New Yorker*. October 19, 2009, 92.

88. It was a lot easier for Prince Hal to step into his father's shoes because Hal had Falstaff to play with and to help him avoid identifying with his father's guilt. Hamlet has only a weak Ophelia as well as a deep sense of disillusion and corruption embodied in Gertrude.

89. For a fuller discussion of dynasty vs. spirit see Philip Fisher, "Thinking about Killing: Hamlet and the Paths among the Passions." *Raritan* X (Summer, 1991).

execute state business efficiently (as in Fortinbras's early threat to the kingdom), but he's a murderer with loose moral standards. Like Macbeth, no one knows his singular stain better than himself:

> O, my offence is rank, it smells to heaven;
> It hath the primal eldest curse upon't ---
> A brother's murder. Pray can I not ....
> O wretched state! O bosom black as death!
> (3.3.36-7)

And what of Gertrude? To which world does she belong? Actually, none of them, and all of them. Like Cleopatra, Gertrude, also a queen, is *sui generis.* She can live in all three worlds, having bedded (or perhaps even seduced) two kings sequentially (and probably simultaneously). She embodies both lust-in-action[90] yet something more universally feminine, something that can retain its hold on a warrior-king after death and attract a jumble of contradictory emotions from the hugely intelligent son she adores but only partly understands. She is one of those *Spectral Women* whose

---

90. Cf. Sonnet 129 ("Th' expense of spirit in a waste of shame....")

ghostly presence haunted Shakespeare's sonnets as well as Antony, Macbeth, Lear, and Othello (but never Bottom).

Polonius, on the other hand, was born to serve a schemer like Claudius. He values only the world of politics, more than even family. His son, Laertes, is a mirror image. As though conspiring, both father and son erect a wall, a Pyramus and Thisbe wall, between Ophelia and Hamlet, the man she loves. As he is leaving to return to Paris, Laertes sternly warns his sister not to give in to Hamlet's "unmaster'd importunity" and lose "your heart, or your chaste treasure." Laertes acknowledges that Hamlet will be king someday, and the most generous "spin" we can give his mini-sermon is that he warns his sister not to end up "despoiled" and have the future king reject her for that reason. Four times he uses the word "fear" in his 34-line admonition.

The significance of this little scene is two-fold. It marks the first time we see Ophelia act with any spunk. She tells Laertes she has understood his homily and squarely positions it in the context of what she knows is his hypocrisy:

> But good my brother,
> Do not as some ungracious pastors do,
> Show me the steep and thorny way to heaven,
> Whiles like a puff'd and reckless libertine
> Himself the primrose path of dalliance treads ....
> (1.3.45-50)

But she is not spunky enough to break free from her family to pursue the only man available to her. Although she is her own person in this dialogue with her older brother, Ophelia becomes increasingly timid as she is acted upon, first by her father, then Hamlet. Following his son's relatively mild warning about Hamlet, Polonius slams the door shut on her relationship with the man she loves:

> I would not, in plain terms, from this time forth
> Have you slander any moment leisure
> As to give words or talk with the Lord Hamlet.
> Look to't, I charge you. (1.3.132.35)

His warning is cast in poisonous terms, telling his daughter that she would "slander" any leisure moments by speaking with the crown prince. Although Polonius casts his advice as for Ophelia's protection, he lets slip the real reason: "Tender yourself more dearly/ Or ... you'll tender me a fool" (1.3.107-109). Like Cassio after Othello discovered him drunk, Polonius's real concern is his reputation, both politically and personally. He is wary of how his daughter will be seen by the court, especially should she become pregnant.

So once again, we have a father breaking trust with his daughter, and not the other way around, as in Fiedler's critique. Old Capulet threatened to throw Juliet out on the street if she didn't agree to his choice of husband. Egeus went farther. He asked the Duke to kill Hermia for the same reason, though we know Shakespeare won't allow that to happen. In a very real sense, what Polonius does to Ophelia is even more egregious. For political purposes, he uses Ophelia as a snare to try to plumb the depths of Hamlet's putative madness:

> *King:* How may we try it further?

Polonius: You know sometimes he walks four hours
             together
        Here in the lobby. ...
        At such a time I'll loose my daughter to him.
                        (2.2.159-62)

"I'll loose my daughter to him." No more despicable words were ever spoken by Pandarus as he "escorts" his niece to her assignation with Troilus. Polonius's using his daughter as sexual bait gives the lie to his advice about being wary of Hamlet's attentions. Ironically, his slimy scheme comes directly from his lecture to Ophelia:

Ophelia: And hath given countenance to his
                    [Hamlet's] speech, my lord,
           With almost all the holy vows of heaven.

Polonius: Ay, springes to catch woodcocks.
                        (1.3.113-15)

I have always wondered why both Laertes and Polonius have blocked Ophelia's path to becoming Queen of Denmark. If Hamlet became king and took Ophelia as wife, would that not solidify Polonius's family's position in Denmark, much less provide Ophelia with a happy and secure future? Both Polonius and Laertes are mistaken in averring that there is an impenetrable class distinction, as Gertrude makes clear during Ophelia's burial: "Sweets to the sweet. Farewell./ I hop'd thou shouldst have been my Hamlet's wife..." (5.1.236-237).

But there is also a collateral consideration, and that is Polonius's personal feelings for his daughter. Once again, we have a father and daughter but no mother. The last meeting of father and daughter alone occurs just after Polonius's instructions to "his man Reynaldo" on how best to spy on Laertes, now back in his favorite Parisian haunts. What Polonius hoped to discover about Laertes and his activities in Paris is not clear; but Polonius obviously is another of Shakespeare's Peeping Toms and another of Claudius's prison guards.[91] After this mini-scene, Polonius neither mentions nor thinks about Laertes again; all his parental care focuses on Ophelia.

As Reynaldo leaves, Ophelia enters, very distressed. "I have been so affrighted," she tells her

91. Both roles reflect Queen Elizabeth's tightly knit surveillance operation, so important to the consolidation of her monarchial power.

father, by a visit from Hamlet during which he said not a word but looked "As if he had been loosed out of hell/ To speak of horrors...."[92] It is as though Hamlet were trying to duplicate the ghost's visitation, and he wanted Ophelia to experience what he had experienced, feel what he had felt. The contrast between his looks and her domesticity could not be starker. Never again will Ophelia be able to do anything happily domestic in her private quarters.

The scene shows us how powerfully the ghost's story of murder and betrayal has affected Hamlet. The ghost is, after all, the *force majeure* in the play, for without him, there would be no play. The scene also tells us that Hamlet had decided to reveal (perhaps even rehearse) his "antic disposition"[93] first on the woman he

---

92. How ironic that Ophelia uses Polonius's own word "loosed"!
93. I have always thought that the genesis of his "antic disposition" was Horatio's warning that the ghost might "tempt you ... to the dreadful summit of the cliff ... and draw you into madness" (1.4.50-55). Stephen Greenblatt ascribes the notion to Saxo's early chronicle in which "Amleth feigned madness, persuading his uncle that he could never pose a danger" ("The Death of Hamnet and the Making of Hamlet.") *The New York Review of Books* LI, 16 (Oct 21, 2004). 44. The two are not mutually exclusive.

loved and had hoped to marry. Perhaps it was his way of trying to let Ophelia "off the hook" gently. He had just spent a harrowing time with his father's ghost. He comes to Ophelia seeking comfort, or companionship, or perhaps just a friendly ear but realizes she is not capable of giving him anything he now needs. In a real sense, the scene represents Hamlet's *adieu* to Ophelia, a companion scene to her brother's most recent *adieu*, warning her not to engage romantically with the Prince. Like so much else about his antic disposition, the results were not what he anticipated. He is play-acting mad, but his visitation is the first step in Ophelia's descent into real madness. Polonius's reactions to his daughter in the next 45 lines (2.1.74-119),"would be scann'd." His first words are, "Mad for thy love?" Surely it is an unusual reaction from a father. It is as though Polonius expected his daughter to relate the details of a pornographic episode, and he was relishing the telling of it.[94] In

---

94. In a real sense, by killing Polonius, Hamlet unwittingly frees Ophelia from the chance of sexual degradation by her father. His nunnery speech is also an attempt to protect Ophelia from the corruption extant in Claudius's court.

response to his "What said he?," Ophelia describes how Hamlet held her by the wrist, stared hard, uttered a piteous sigh, and then left her closet without taking his eyes off her.

By his next response, "Come, go with me, I will go seek the King," Polonius makes clear that his political standing matters most, not his daughter's disconcerting experience. Ophelia tells her father that "as you did command," she "denied/ His access to me." Here is Polonius's puzzling response:

That hath made him mad.
　I am sorry that with better heed and judgment
　I had not quoted (i.e., observed) him. I fear'd he did
　but trifle
　And meant to wrack thee. But beshrew my jealousy! [95]

---

95. In the last three years I have seen ten productions of Hamlet. Only one of them (the recent Donmar Warehouse production, starring Jude Law) cuts this line, and only one gives any gloss. In Shakespeare & Company's (Lenox, MA) August 26, 2009 production, Polonius's body language during this scene makes clear that while he is probably not thinking (or capable) of incest, he is, at the least, a lecherous old man. In Kenneth Branagh's 1996 film, he makes the same point by showing a floozy in Polonius's bedroom while the old man is instructing Reynaldo. I am not sure what Polonius means by "jealousy." Does he use the word much as it is used in Othello or simply as "anger" or "wrath"? The OED cites seven definitions, with several sub-sections.

By heaven, it is as proper to our age
To cast beyond ourselves in our opinions

As it is common for the younger sort
To lack discretion. (2.1.110-17)

Is Polonius apologizing for demanding that Ophelia cut off all contact with Hamlet? He seems to say he was afraid Hamlet was not serious and meant "to wrack thee," that is, to injure or cause her downfall. It is not clear whether Polonius also intended any sexual meaning (like rape, for example). Or, is he saying that it now turns out Hamlet *was* serious, and the closed door to Ophelia's "access" has "made him mad?" If so, Polonius takes no action to help his daughter and reverse his harsh order and, in fact, seems to offer only the feeble excuse that old men take extreme positions much as young people act without discretion. We are reduced to thinking that the father is always jealous of the son-in-law or the prospective son-in-law.

I very much like George Lyman Kittredge's (the old master's) gloss on this scene and do hereby quote much of it: "It is at this moment that Hamlet decides that he must renounce Ophelia and give up all thoughts of marriage and happiness. To involve an innocent girl in such a revenge as he contemplates would have been a crime. His study of Ophelia's face is but the long look in which he says farewell to his hopes.... Hamlet cannot for a moment have wished to make Ophelia his accomplice in a deed of blood."[96]

This scene also establishes that the breach in Hamlet's relationship with Ophelia was initiated by her, under strict orders from Polonius. When the father-daughter bond was broken, neither Hermia, Portia, nor Jessica paid with her life. Juliet and Ophelia do, as will Desdemona. Nor do fathers escape scot free. Old Capulet is severely reprimanded by the Prince and has lost his only heir, Egeus is simply brushed aside, Shylock is disgraced in public (and must turn Christian), Brabantio will die of a broken heart, and in *Hamlet,* Polonius becomes the victim of his own "springe." In

96. George Lyman Kittredge, ed. *The Tragedy of Hamlet.* Boston, Ginn (1939), 178.

Shakespeare, there is no universal formula for father-daughter rupture, but the horrendous consequences of generic familial schism will have to wait for *King Lear,* while its repair, the return to healing, forgiveness, and reconciliation, will have to wait for *The Winter's Tale,* five and ten years later, respectively.

The scene leads thematically (if not directly) to the nunnery scene. As soon as Hamlet learns that his father was murdered by his uncle and that his mother played fast and loose with his father, he views Ophelia as a potential Gertrude. After asking her if she is "honest" and "fair," comes this exchange:

Ophelia: What means your lordship?

Hamlet: That if you be honest and fair, your honesty should
Admit no discourse to your beauty.

Ophelia: Could beauty, my lord, have better commerce than
With honesty?

Hamlet: Ay, truly, for the power of beauty will sooner transform honesty from

what it is to a bawd than the
force of honesty can translate beauty
into his likeness.
This was sometime a paradox, but now the
time gives it proof. (3.1.106-15)

This repeats what the ghost says happened to his "most
seeming-virtuous queen." Hamlet tells Ophelia that
"now," that is, in Claudius's corrupt Denmark, beauty
turns honesty into something not just dishonest but
downright bawdy. To Hamlet, Ophelia has become a
young Gertrude, and there is no way Hamlet wants that
kind of marriage, "stew'd in corruption" and "breeding
maggots." There is only one solution for Ophelia, whom
Hamlet still loves: "Get thee to a nunnery," because in
Claudius's Denmark, "be thou as chaste as ice, as pure as
snow, thou shalt not escape calumny." Ophelia probably
has little idea what Hamlet is telling her.

By 1600, however, the rough date of this play's
composition, there were no more nunneries in England.
As part of Henry's VIII's break with Rome and
assumption of leadership of the Church of England,
between 1536 and 1541 he disbanded monasteries,

priories, convents, and friaries in England, Wales, and Ireland. The impact on former nuns was devastating, and some of them ended up earning a living as prostitutes. Partly as a result of these developments, the word "nunnery" became slang for "bawdy house," especially in third rate dramas of the time. We can choose to ignore this bawdy, slangish meaning, but we cannot ignore Hamlet's labeling Polonius a fishmonger, or a procurer. Nor can we discount Hamlet's denunciation of Ophelia as a bawdy surrogate of all women.

Although not as vicious as he was with his mother, Hamlet *does* attack Ophelia, coming close to labeling her a whore. "You jig and amble, and you lisp, you nickname God's creatures, and make your wantonness your ignorance. Go to, I'll no more on't, it hath made me mad." We have never seen Ophelia jig, amble, lisp, give nicknames to animals, or act wantonly. Hamlet is in high dudgeon, and poor Ophelia must endure his hot-tempered assault. And then, the *coup de grace*: "I say we will have no mo marriage. Those that are married already – all but one – shall live; the rest shall keep as they are. To a nunnery, go" (3.1.146-151). In Hamlet's mind, revenge and marriage are coupled, as are Gertrude and Ophelia. But to Claudius, hiding behind a curtain, Hamlet's words constitute a direct threat, and the king immediately decides to send Hamlet to England with an urgent request that the English king kill the son of the brother he murdered.

Try as she will, Ophelia does not understand this change in their relationship, nor does she have the inner resources Gertrude has. Hamlet has not given her the key to his puzzle, as he will soon give Gertrude, and Ophelia believes he has gone mad. She becomes "of ladies most deject and wretched …. O woe is me/ T'have seen what I have seen, see what I see." She has taken the penultimate step in her slide into depression ("most deject"). Soon her father will be killed and buried "hugger mugger." Her brother is far away in Paris, her lover's mind "here o'erthrown," and when he leaves Denmark for England, what is left for Ophelia? Her father has closed her door to Hamlet, who now verbally attacks her, for reasons she cannot understand.

In *Hamlet,* Ophelia inherits the weedy mantle of earlier daughters – of Juliet and Thisbe – all three are young women who, through no fault of their own, encounter life's formidable traps and, unable to find a way out, die. Worse yet, Ophelia takes unto herself the ill fortunes of others. Hamlet pretends he is mad; Ophelia goes mad. Hamlet is sent to England over the seas, ostensibly to his death; Ophelia drowns in a nearby stream. Polonius is buried "hugger mugger," and so is Ophelia. For Ophelia, drowning represents her return to a loving, enveloping, accepting maternal presence. Her mother is gone, and she will not find a surrogate in Gertrude.

But did she commit suicide? The gravedigger said "she willfully" sought "her own salvation" (5.1.1-2). And Hamlet remarked to Horatio on the "maimed rites" and said, "This doth betoken/ The corse they follow did with desp'rate hand/ Fordo it own life" (5.1.212-214), the clear implication of the Priest's reply to Laertes's "What ceremony else?"

The only account of her death is spoken by Gertrude, who interrupts Claudius and Laertes's plotting. She speaks as though she were an eye witness, and what she describes is clearly an accident – as a distracted Ophelia was placing flowers on a stream-side branch, it broke:

> There on the pendent boughs her crownet weeds
> Clamb'ring to hang, an envious sliver broke,
> When down her weedy trophies and herself
> Fell in the weeping brook. (4.7.171-74)

To my mind, the issue lies unresolved except that it would be typical of her fate for Hamlet to ponder suicide, "To be or not to be," and for her to execute it. In either case, her support system fades away, and her young, fragile mind then leaves this world and sinks to the world below.

In her desperation, she seeks the mother she lacks but is first refused admission to Gertrude: "I will not speak with her." Gertrude's reluctance to see Ophelia is

born of guilt:

> To my sick soul, as sin's true nature is,
> Each toy seems prologue to some great amiss.
> So full of artless jealousy is guilt,
> It spills itself in fearing to be spilt. (4.5.17-20)

Like blood spreading from a punctured vein, Old

Hamlet's murder has now turned Gertrude's soul sick,

just as it did Claudius's. Now they are, willy-nilly, in bed

together. Gertrude's guilt stems from her complicity in

Claudius and Polonius's conspiracy to berate Hamlet for

his behavior at "The Mousetrap." She allowed Polonius

to hide in her bedroom chamber, where he did not

belong. If Ophelia came to ask, "How was it my father

was killed in your private suite?", what would she have

said? Her four-line confession also signals that Hamlet's

verbal assault on his mother hit home. When she

pleaded, "O speak to me no more./ These words like

daggers enter in my ears."[97] And, "O Hamlet, thou hast cleft my heart in twain," she meant it.

Ophelia's opening line in the scene is perhaps the play's saddest: "Where is the beauteous Majesty of Denmark?" (4.5.21). She seeks comfort. Her father is dead, her lover might as well be, and her brother is far away, in a foreign land. She has no nurse, like Juliet, no handmaidens, like Cleopatra. She is dreadfully alone in a world she no longer understands. But there is no way Gertrude can comfort Ophelia, whose mind has become unhinged; Gertrude needs comforting herself. Ophelia croons six sad songs about the death of her father and the death of her lover. She sings to Gertrude, another sad lady who lost her true love then found another:

How should I your true love know
From another one?...
He is dead and gone, lady ...
At his heels a stone. (4.5.22-23, 32)

---

97. An echo of the "leperous distilment" that Claudius poured into old Hamlet's ears.

She also sings of Saint Valentine's Day, when a young man greets a young girl at his chamber window, and she loses her "chaste treasure":

Then up he rose, and donn'd his clo'es,
And dupp'd the chamber door,
Let in the maid that out a maid
 Never departed more. (4.5.52-5)

Both Laertes and Polonius have warned Ophelia about losing her virginity: "or your chaste treasure open/ To his unmaster'd importunity" (1.3.31-32) and, "Tender yourself more dearly/ Or … you'll tender me a fool" (1.3.107-109). Twice in Kenneth Branagh's film there are brief flashback scenes showing Hamlet and Ophelia making love, both quite naked. So perhaps this song of Saint Valentine, from Branagh's viewpoint, hints that Ophelia was pregnant by Hamlet, adding one more mental albatross dragging poor Ophelia's mind under water.[98]

---

98. In a June, 2010, performance at The Folger Theatre, at the end of her first made scene, Ophelia turns to the audience, parts her gown, and pats her big belly. She exits stage left with, "I hope all will be well," giving us a new meaning for that line.

For Ophelia, Gertrude *is* "the beauteous Majesty," both because that is probably an accurate physical description and because somewhere deep inside, Ophelia must have nurtured a wish to succeed Gertrude. For the ghost, however, "the beauteous Majesty of Denmark" turned out to be "my most seeming-virtuous queen." The ghost tells Hamlet a tale both of brotherly murder, "most foul, strange and unnatural," and of wifely surrender to Claudius's "shameful lust."

> So lust, though to a radiant angel link'd,
> Will sate itself in a celestial bed
> And prey on garbage....
> Let not the royal bed of Denmark be
> A couch for luxury and damned incest. (1.5.55-83)

The ghost's language – "Let not the royal bed of Denmark" – forces Hamlet to imagine his mother in bed with his uncle and that image revolts him. It corrupts his thinking about Ophelia – "I say we will have no mo marriage" – and about Gertrude. Hamlet's assignation with his ghost-father haunts him throughout the first half of the play, coming into sharp focus during his interview with his mother, in her closet (3.4). To prepare the queen for her meeting with Hamlet, Polonius urges, "Pray you be round." But, ironically, it is Hamlet who is "round," even merciless, with his mother:

Queen: Have you forgot me?

Hamlet: No, by the rood, not so.
           You are the Queen, your husband's
                      brother's wife,
           And, would it were not so, you are my
                      mother.

[At this point, Hamlet kills Polonius, hoping it is the King.]

Queen: O what a rash and bloody deed is this!

Hamlet: A bloody deed. Almost as bad, good mother,
           As kill a king and marry with his brother.

Queen: As kill a king?

Hamlet: Ay, lady, it was my word.

As though accidentally killing Polonius was just a footnote to Gertrude's evil deeds, Hamlet forges ahead.

Queen:	What have I done, that thou dar'st wag thy tongue
	In noise so rude against me?

Hamlet:	Such an act
	That blurs the grace and blush of modesty,
	Calls virtue hypocrite ...
	Makes marriage vows
	As false as dicers' oaths. (3.4.10-45)

Hamlet accuses her of adultery, of incest, and of being an accessory to murder,[99] and then skewers her by saying he wishes she were not his mother. He brands Claudius "a murderer and a villain ... a king of shreds and patches," that is, someone who wears motley and is no better than a fool. How ironic! Hamlet has just become a murderer and with his "antic disposition" does himself play the fool. He tells his mother she has stopped mourning Hyperion and now consorts with the satyr "to live/ In the rank sweat of an enseamed bed,/ Stew'd in

---

99. Gertrude's rejoinder to Hamlet's accusation, in line 29, "As kill a king?" establishes her innocence. She has no knowledge of Claudius's murder of her first husband. Hamlet seems to ignore her demurral and forges ahead berating his mother.

corruption, honeying and making love/ Over the nasty sty!"[100]

What a scene! Gertrude cowers under her son's relentless attack until, like the Lone Ranger riding to the rescue, the ghost reappears, visible to Hamlet only, "to whet thy almost blunted purpose." Perhaps the ghost noticed that in "The Mousetrap," partly written and wholly staged by his son, the player King was not killed by his brother but by Lucianus, "nephew to the King." In other words, the play-within-the-play stages Hamlet's *desire* to kill Claudius, to obey his father's dread command. At this stage Hamlet is capable only of producing a play, staging a fiction. The ghost's final words to his son are, "Remember me," that is, "Remember your promised revenge; remember your father who came from the world of action, not of philosophizing." And then the ghost disappears from the

_____

100. Perhaps Hamlet's bedroom counsel to Gertrude parallels his deep desire for "honeying and making love" with Ophelia, now no longer possible.

play.[101] In this scene, Shakespeare intends to solidify in our minds the coupling of revenge and marriage, Gertrude's marriage.[102] Both are unsavory.

A mere seven lines after discovering that the person behind the arras was not Claudius,[103] Hamlet renews his attack, though somewhat more gently, as the ghost had implored. Ringing in Hamlet's head is the ghost's imprecation, "Let not the royal bed of Denmark be/ A couch for luxury and damned incest." The royal bed produced only one child and clearly did not satisfy Gertrude, else she would not have been tempted by Claudius, who, as old Hamlet's younger brother, would have been a frequent visitor. What else was there for

---

101. In the 2004 RSC production in Stratford, England, whenever the ghost appears he drags a broadsword behind him, clinking and clanging over a metal grate. It's a haunting noise. As the final lights go down, the last noise the audience hears is the clanging of the ghost's sword. (Source: *The Shakespeare Newsletter*. Summer/Fall 2004, 64)

102. In his Introduction to the Arden Hamlet, Harold Jenkins emphasizes how important this coupling is to Hamlet's state of mind and to his actions. Jenkins's entire Introduction is intelligent, persuasive, and beautifully written.

103. When Hamlet sees that the body is Polonius's, his exclamation, "I took thee for thy better," at first glance makes sense. He would not expect the king's prime minister to be in his mother's bedroom suite but would expect her husband to be there. On the other hand, Hamlet had just left Claudius "downstairs," praying. Was there a private elevator?

him to do? If old Hamlet had been cannier, he would have put his brother in command of a division of troops, and put him in the front line, as the wily Octavius placed Antony's defectors "that Antony may seem to spend his fury/ Upon himself" (*Antony and Cleopatra*, 4.6.10-11).

Hamlet entreats his mother to "sit you down" so he can emblazon on her memory the portraits of her two husbands, another use of mirrors. One had "Hyperion's curls, the front of Jove himself,/ An eye like Mars..." the other is "a king of shreds and patches." Did old Hamlet, as Mars, spend too much time away from Elsinore, fighting wars (some seemingly on sleds), leaving Gertrude home to become a desperate housewife? Hamlet sarcastically tells his mother, "You cannot call it love; for at your age/ The heyday in the blood is tame...." Well, we're not so sure. Cleopatra was not young, yet her libido, her "blood's heyday," came to Antony full-blown.[104] And Hamlet himself describes his

---

104. For example, "Or is he on his horse?/ O happy horse, to bear the weight of Antony" (1.5.20-21).

mother as "honeying and making love/ Over the nasty sty," not very "tame" at all!

Was Hamlet jealous of Claudius, Oedipus-like, as Iago claimed to be of Othello? Or was Gertrude's lusty behavior so obvious that this is simply an accurate characterization? Perhaps, indeed, Gertrude was both a "trophy wife," much younger than old Hamlet, as well as a woman with unrelenting sexual needs, like Goneril and Regan, both concupiscent and both about the same age as Gertrude. Circe-like, Gertrude was courted and bedded by two kings, sequentially and perhaps simultaneously. So, whether or not her complexion was dark, she is another Dark Lady of the sonnets, living now in Elsinore, consorting and marrying first old Hamlet and then, while old Hamlet was still king, seducing or being seduced by his brother. To cement the parallel, Hamlet is the poet, his father his special friend, and Claudius the rival who also succumbs to the Dark Lady's allure, much to the distress of the poet (i.e., Hamlet). She is that "terrifying spectre ... in the shape of a nightmare: the woman who is in fact untrue to her vows as a lover,"[105] the woman who "makes marriage vows/ As false as dicers' oaths." It seems that Shakespeare could not shake from his imagination this pattern from the sonnets or the guilt that enslaved the poet, in this case Hamlet. So while the inexorable working out of the vortex of the Dark Lady and other aspects of fate ensnared Hamlet, Claudius, Gertrude, Laertes, and Polonius, not to mention Rosencrantz and Guildenstern,

---

105. Richard Wheeler has an interesting gloss on "the spectral woman," who may or may not be the Dark Lady: "All these plays are haunted by an image of woman that no particular female character can embody. Some of her traits are approximated in different ways in Regan and Goneril, in Lady Macbeth, in Cressida, and in others. But the idea of woman that paralyzes Hamlet's will is never identical with Gertrude, certainly not with Ophelia, just as the woman whose sulphurous pit Lear rages against at Dover is not identical with, and does not come into existence with, Regan and Goneril – though they, like Cordelia, are deeply implicated in his fierce revulsion. The experience of the tragic protagonist is shaped by an imaginary specter of woman, outside the masculine order of law, who seduces, betrays, usurps, castrates, who melts Hamlet's virtue (virtu), who releases the tears that scald Lear "upon a wheel of fire" (IV.vii.47), who puts Othello's manhood at the mercy of "every puny whispster" (V.ii.245). She is an imaginary woman who ultimately demands death, and from whom life can be freed only by tragic action that sacrifices the most manly of men – and often the best of women – to her. She is the woman for whom Othello mistakes Desdemona, and whom he thinks he can kill by murdering his wife." Wheeler, 150.

the saddest victim of all is Ophelia, whose love for both her father and her lover was misplaced and mistreated.

■ *Othello*

My story being done
She gave me for my pains a world of sighs ...
And bade me, if I had a friend that loved her,
I should but teach him how to tell my story
And that would woo her.

The better angel is a man right fair,
The worser spirit a woman colored ill. (Son. 144)

If *Hamlet* is a play of mirrors, *Othello* is a play replete with questions. What was there about Iago that drew Othello to him, especially as Othello had just bypassed him for promotion? Why did Cassio, after his drunken disgrace, not use his wit and charm to appeal directly to Othello? After all, he had in some manner helped Othello woo Desdemona. What was there about Othello that attracted Desdemona? Why, in her distress, does Desdemona turn to acidic Iago for help, calling him "good friend"? And perhaps we should begin with this:

Why was Desdemona seemingly so eager to leave home, country, and father?

Near the end of the play, after Desdemona and Emilia have recognized a great change in Othello's mien, Emilia bemoans,

> Hath she forsook so many noble matches,
> Her father, and her country, and her friends,
> To be called whore? (4.2.127-29)

"So many noble matches"? Well, perhaps, but the only suitor we know about is Roderigo, and when he and Iago have roused Desdemona's father from sleep, Brabantio clearly tells him, "My daughter is not for thee" (1.1.97). In the verbal brawl that follows, Roderigo, not Iago, convinces Brabantio that he may have a problem with his daughter. He tells the senator that she has hired a gondolier to bring her "to the gross clasps of a lascivious Moor" and has "made a gross revolt,/ Tying her duty, beauty, wit and fortunes" to "an extravagant and wheeling stranger." It is Roderigo's only sensible speech (1.1.118-138). For those of us (in the audience) who fell in love with Desdemona, we vainly wish she could have heard Othello described as "an extravagant and wheeling stranger." Perhaps she would have had second thoughts. Roderigo goes on to tell Brabantio that if he is wrong, he should be punished, but if correct, Brabantio should give heed to his warning. From then on, he places his purse and his lust for Desdemona into Iago's hands and receives, in compensation, a fatal stab wound from his patron.

Perhaps Emilia exaggerated when she said, "so many noble matches." But surely she accurately noted that Desdemona has forsaken her father. So we are once again encountering a story in which a daughter turns away from her father and, in the end, dies. Why does she die? Is it *because* she leaves her father? In one sense, Yes. Can this beautiful young Venetian virgin be a witch? Othello calls her a strumpet and a whore. Brabantio accuses Othello of witchcraft. Are they both mistaken?

In the play's very first action, Brabantio is rudely awakened by Roderigo and Iago who warn him "an old black ram/ Is tupping your white ewe!" Despite Brabantio's initial denial that his daughter could be missing, he suspected that something was amiss: "This accident is not unlike my dream,/ Belief of it oppresses me already" (1.1.140-141). What was wrong between father and daughter that crept into Brabantio's dream? Ironically, it was Brabantio who "oft invited" Othello to his house. For Brabantio, Othello was that "extravagant and wheeling stranger," an entertainer who loved to tell tales of his exotic travels:

> ... of the cannibals that each other eat,[106]
> The Anthropophagi, and men whose heads
> Do grow beneath their shoulders. (1.3.144-46)

Early on, Othello might be viewed as a male Scheherazade, able to spin story after story to avoid execution. One wonders whether Shakespeare knew this folk tale, whose plot begins with a king who killed his bride because of her infidelity, so ironically foreshadowing Desdemona's fate. Janet Adelman calls

---

106. A cruel foreshadowing of Iago, who will plant the jealousy that will devour Othello.

Othello "a type of the *miles gloriosus* [boastful soldier],"[107] prompting us to doubt the veracity of so many of Othello's exotic yarns

Brabantio probably enjoyed many of Othello's stories, whether or not he believed there were cannibals who ate each other and "men whose heads/ Did grow beneath their shoulders." And what did Desdemona think of this accomplished storyteller? As a wordsmith, Othello is Hamlet grown old and foolish, thinking he can satisfy this accomplished, young Venetian. Words are his undoing. He wooed her with his exotic tales and then was himself wooed by Iago's prolix prevarications about his wife's being tupped by his lieutenant, whom he had just promoted to prominence.

We know little about Desdemona's home life. As a senator, perhaps Brabantio was not often home and not able to devote as much time to Desdemona as he'd like, so Othello's various visits helped enliven his household and clearly captivated his daughter. There was no Mrs. Brabantio, nor does Desdemona anywhere

---

107. Adelman, 51.

reminisce about her mother. Under those circumstances, we can wonder about incest, as in *Pericles,* or a languorous desire, or simply an understandable paternal possessiveness, a milder Polonius without any political ambition. We can only speculate about what Brabantio's dream meant; Desdemona's elopement brought something to the surface of Brabantio's mind that "oppresses me already." Or maybe Desdemona simply found life at home with Dad boring, so when the swashbuckling warrior came to visit and spun larger-than-life narratives, she saw an opportunity to escape to what might be a more exciting life. And exciting it was, but not the way Desdemona dreamed.

Othello's version is that during many of his storytelling visits, Desdemona would have to excuse herself because "the house affairs would draw her thence...," but soon she'd return, eager to hear more. She had "a greedy ear" to "devour up my discourse." And then, according to Othello, she dropped a broad hint:

She thanked me
And bade me, if I had a friend that loved her,
I should but teach him how to tell my story
And that would woo her. Upon this hint I spake:
She loved me for the dangers I had passed
And I loved her that she did pity them.

(1.3.164-69)

The initiative seems to be Desdemona's, so often the case in Shakespeare. Is that a Romeo and Juliet romance? Or even a lustful Troilus and Cressida? "She loved me for the dangers I had passed." That line is the play's clearest indication of how young Desdemona is. Her attraction sounds like hero-worship, much like today's teen-age girl waiting at the stage door for an autograph from Jude Law, fresh from the evening's performance of *Hamlet*. Of course, Othello loved having such an attentive audience. Had Othello ever before such an adoring devotee? Probably not. His is the world of men and politics and war and not Cassio's Florentine world of civilized social intercourse.

But Othello is not Antony or Hector or Prince Hal. As Carol Neely astutely points out, the "travailous history" he enjoyed telling "describes, when closely examined, what he has suffered rather than what he has done."[108] What we see in this scene is an older man, a homeless nomad, someone who had to endure much, including being sold into slavery and somehow redeemed. When he meets Desdemona, his reputation is at its peak, and the Venetian rulers clearly want him in charge to fend off the anticipated Turkish attack on Cyprus, a situation resonating with Shakespeare's audience's memory of the feared Spanish invasion of 1588.

In the key scene in Act One, before the Duke and the assembled senators, acting as a kind of street jury, Brabantio establishes the ground rules: "If she confess that she was half the wooer,/ Destruction on my head if my bad blame/ Light on the man" (1.3.176-178). And then, uncharacteristically calling his daughter "gentle

---

108. Carol Thomas Neely, "Women and Men in Othello: 'what should such a fool/ Do with so good a woman?'" *Shakespeare Studies* 10 (1977), 146.

mistress,"[109] father asks daughter to declare "where most you owe obedience." The question demonstrates how ill prepared Brabantio is to lose his daughter and to adjust to the reality of what he sees right in front of him – Desdemona married to Othello. It's both a prelude to Lear's defining question and a reprise of Egeus's complaint to Theseus about his daughter's disobedience in choosing a mate. Both Egeus and Brabantio lose the contest, but in *A Midsummer Night's Dream,* we instinctively know that fun and games will follow, not tragedy and death. Desdemona's first words respond specifically to her being "half the wooer": "I do perceive here a divided duty," divided, that is, *exactly* in half!

Brabantio realizes he's been outflanked by the Moor *and* his daughter. In Venice, Desdemona and Othello are partnered, acting together as they never will again. They cooperate to help Desdemona leave her father and his household. Despite his dream (or perhaps

---

109. The Arden edition footnotes this phrase at l. 178 with: "gentle mistress is not how a father normally addressed his daughter," again raising the spectre of incest.

because of it), Brabantio does not understand why she would "Run from her guardage to the sooty bosom/ Of such a thing as thou," as though Othello were Caliban.

Like Old Capulet, at first he praises his daughter:

A maiden never bold,
Of spirit so still and quiet that her motion
Blushed at herself…. (1.3.95-7)

But then, also just like Capulet, he turns his back on his only heir, although not so savagely. Instead, Brabantio abandons fatherhood by default: "I had rather to adopt a child than get it." And so in Act One, Desdemona, because she abandons her father's household, precipitates her father's abandonment of her, and both lose the opportunity for a reciprocal relationship of love and trust.

What is it with these Elizabethan fathers, Capulet, Egeus and Brabantio? Do they have eyes only for sons, not recognizing that the sole potential for new life lies with their daughters? In my ancient (1963) Shakespeare Concordance, there is only one citation for "grandchild," and that in *Coriolanus,* a relatively late play. Was

Shakespeare so wedded to Elizabethan custom that he saw only paternal disdain whenever a daughter didn't slavishly kowtow to dad's choice of mate? Or was this grand master of dissection experimenting with the father-daughter covenant as he went along, waiting for his ever restless and creative spirit to fashion a Perdita, lost at first but returning home at last, and a Miranda, whose wondrous spirit nursed her preceptor of a father with the milk of trusting reciprocal love?

So with the drama barely underway, Desdemona loses the support of her only parent. Before departing Venice, she must also somehow confront one more problem. Her husband is a Moor, a black man. *Othello* was written in 1604, a time when, according to Shakespearean scholar Daniel Vitkus, for English society "black skin color was understood ... primarily with a symbolic logic." "What blackness symbolized then was evil and barbarity, the unknown from the wilds of North

Africa washed up on the shores of civilization."[110] The black-white contrast, perhaps even contest, is crudely introduced in the first scene by Iago, bellowing up at Brabantio,[111] telling him he has "lost half your soul" because "now, very now, an old black ram/ Is tupping your white ewe" (1.1.86-88). As though Brabantio doesn't quite understand the animal imagery's consequence, Iago warns him that he is danger of inheriting grandchildren who will be part horses: "You'll have your nephews neigh to you, you'll have coursers for cousins and jennets for germans!" At this inference of miscegenation, Brabantio, now fully awake, retorts, "What profane wretch art thou?" (1.1.111-113). Sadly, Brabantio's cuttingly accurate description helps neither him nor Roderigo escape the poisoned tentacles of the play's truly black character.

So now Desdemona has two strikes against her. But there is yet a third, and, of course, it is Iago who

---

110. From Hilton Als's review of Peter Sellars October, 2009, production of *Othello*. The first quoted sentence is by Vitkus, the second by Als, in the October 5, 2009, *The New Yorker*, 86.
111. Is this a Shakespearean balcony scene satire?

gives the signal: "An *old* black ram." At least thrice Othello himself reinforces the distinction: "the young affects/ In me defunct..." (1.3.264-265); his scorn for "light-winged toys/ Of feathered Cupid" (1.3.269-270); and, "for I am declined/ Into the vale of years..." (3.3.269-270). In his Arden edition Introduction, E.A.J. Honigmann asserts that "there are many hints that Desdemona is meant to be very young, almost childlike...."[112] It's an important point because it throws light on why Brabantio was so upset when she leaves his household, with Othello or anyone, on why Desdemona was so passive to Othello's threats, and on the question of whether their marriage was ever consummated. Metaphorically, it could not have been, for Othello was castrated, both by Iago and by his jealous rage. Perhaps Desdemona saw him more as a father figure than as a lover. And if she was so much younger, unlike Gertrude, Cleopatra, or Juliet, Desdemona may have been reluctant to face that defining womanly moment. And

---

112. E.A.J. Honigmann, ed., *The Arden Shakespeare Othello*. London, Thomson Learning (2006), 41.

Othello, for his part, was not eager to demonstrate his less than manly bedroom performance. Is Desdemona the first woman Othello slept with – or didn't sleep with?

Juliet met, married, and would have run away with a stranger. Somehow we feel that it could have worked, but for the father and the feud. Youth would have prevailed. Desdemona does the same, yet somehow, when this January-May couple sails off to Cyprus, their departing in separate vessels semaphores that this honeymoon will not bond this couple but only widen the breach. So the defining question underlying everything that happens in Act One is this: Can Desdemona, through the sheer beauty of her intention, hold on to the husband she knew in Venice just long enough to create a happy marriage in Cyprus? Is she, much like Rosalind, a skillful enough painter to mix the white with the black to create in her palette something as lovely as the pearl of an oyster?

In Shakespeare, sea voyages are always transformative. In *Othello,* the voyage to Cyprus changes everything. In leaving her father's household, Desdemona pairs her interests with her brand new husband's. No longer will he spin fantastic yarns to her rapt attention, except the one that will prove deadly – the one about the handkerchief. In Venice, Othello was smiling and patient, and Desdemona was in charge. In the scene before the Duke and the senators, it's Desdemona's speech about "divided duty" that both turns off her father and saves her husband from jail. And when it's clear Othello must immediately leave for Cyprus, Desdemona is equally clear that she won't stay behind, especially not at her father's house. Her words are provocative:

> Nor would I there reside
> To put my father in impatient thoughts
> By being in his eye. (1.3.242-4)

What would Brabantio have been "impatient" about – that he lost his daughter to someone else, or that she ran off with the Moor, or both?

Once in Cyprus, Othello metamorphoses precisely into what Vitkus wrote "black" symbolizes: "evil and barbarity" (see page 163). He turns suspicious and nasty, as though fulfilling Brabantio's accusation that he operates via "spells and medicines bought of mountebanks" and practices witchcraft – the husband as witch and not the daughter. He calls his wife "that cunning whore of Venice" (4.2.91) and even strikes her in public (4.1.239), thus abandoning any pretence that she is his adored partner. Instead, he treats her as though she were a recent recruit under his command, someone he can slap around at will, perhaps as he was treated when a slave, during his former life of "chaos."

Cassio's lament about the impact of drink now applies also to Othello, who has become intoxicated by Iago: "To be now a sensible man, by and by a fool, and presently a beast" (2.3.300-301), and it is Othello the beast who strikes his young bride. Ironically, Cassio is the one man who unerringly treats Desdemona with respect. He calls her "The divine Desdemona" (2.1.73). But even he degenerates to common man (like Roderigo and Iago) when dealing with Bianca, his amazingly loyal courtesan. When it comes to healing the breach between him and Othello, this silver-tongued man mysteriously turns to Iago for advice, so shortly after Iago's exhortation about drink led Cassio to disaster. Why does everyone turn to Iago for help and advice and act *against* his or her best interest? Iago's talent for seeming to emphasize captures and defeats everyone. Cassio's attempt to influence his boss indirectly, through Desdemona, is the cornerstone that seals Desdemona's cruel fate. On Cyprus, Cassio's instinct for courtesy and respect is turned inside out.

What is going on between Othello and Iago? Despite bypassing Iago for Cassio, all of Othello's masculine attention is lavished on Iago whom he unnaturally chooses as his confidant. This decision immediately casts doubt on Othello's judgment. Why favor the man you just demoted? Once on Cyprus, Othello's fantasy of Desdemona's infidelity quite emasculates him, leading us to wonder how manly he really is. If he is the accomplished warrior he tells us (and has apparently convinced the Venetian senators of), and if that is supposed to indicate manliness, why does that evaporate before the prospect of woman's sexual infidelity? Ironically, he is the first to recognize it. To Iago he sings his twelve-line farewell to arms song: "Farewell the tranquil mind.... Farewell the plumed troops ... and the neighing steed ... the royal banner ... Pride, pomp and circumstance of glorious war! ... Othello's occupation's gone" (3.3.360). Robbed of whatever testosterone he had left, Othello is now prey to more than just jealousy. He and Iago both exhibit "a troubled masculine response to women."[113] They have both, as Neely has written, come to "see the women as whores and then refuse to tolerate their own projections... [while] the women fatally overestimate the men." Both sexes "badly misunderstand each other."[114]

Othello and Iago are, then, in this sense, twinned, so different from Antonio and Bassanio, each of whom showed a gentle affection for the other. So, too, are Roderigo and Cassio twinned, neither of whom can

---

113. Wheeler, 128.
114. Neely, 148.

pursue his goals but through the intermediation of Iago. Curiously, Othello is as easily duped as both, showing (again) how foolish and weak-willed this allegedly great general is. Iago performs a *trifecta* of deceit, and Othello comes in dead last. In anticipation of Othello's farewell anthem, Iago, reprising Claudius, vows, "I'll pour this pestilence into his ear" (2.3.351), sensing that more than Othello's ears are now susceptible to the penetration of contagion. Othello is Iago's superior, his "boss," and surely part of Iago's motivation is to intoxicate his boss, to bring Othello down to his level, just as he did with Cassio. The bearer of jealousy is himself jealous, and his attempt to infect Othello is, in a very real sense, an attempt to off-load his sickness onto his boss and thus cleanse himself. And so Iago injects the green monster of jealousy into Othello in a manner that can only be described as symbolic sodomy. Here's how:

During his seemingly endless attempt to convince Othello he has been cuckolded, Iago relates to Othello this imaginary and grotesque episode:

I lay with Cassio lately
And being troubled with a raging tooth
I could not sleep....
In sleep I heard him say 'Sweet Desdemona,
Let us be wary, let us hide our loves,'
And then, sir, would he gripe and wring my hand,
Cry 'O sweet creature!' and then kiss me hard
As if he plucked up kisses by the roots
That grew upon my lips, lay his leg o'er my thigh,
And sigh, and kiss .... (3.3.416-427)

It's so outrageous that Iago must know that only a dupe would believe it, unless Iago has another purpose in mind – a dark, subconscious desire. Iago's deeper ulterior motive involves telling Othello what he calls this "dream" because he can't own up to wishing to have such a romp himself with Othello. It's what Freud would call "transference" and is followed by another bizarre scene in which the partners kneel to each other and execute a black mass and a black marriage. Othello invokes "black vengeance, from the hollow hell" in order to fill his bosom with "aspics' tongues." Iago conjures "you ever-burning lights above" to "Witness that here

Iago doth give up/ The execution of his wit, hands, heart,/ To wronged Othello's service." And when Iago promises to kill Cassio, the ceremony ends thus:

Othello: Now art thou my lieutenant.

Iago: I am your own for ever.

(3.3.450-482, passim).

As though to consummate this marriage, in contrast to Othello's with Desdemona, Act Four opens with each of the partners discussing what it means to be naked in bed and to lie "with her" or "on her." In much the same manner, some years hence, Leontes will be so disturbed by seeing his queen exchange the kind of intimacies with his old friend that he envies but knows are prohibited by society, Othello is so disturbed by his new intimacy with Iago that he is reduced to a kind of babbling idiot in prose (4.1.35-43), perhaps even foaming at the mouth, before collapsing into an epileptic fit. His last words are, "O devil!" by which he means Desdemona but subconsciously also brands Iago.

Without the epilepsy scene, we might be tempted to view Othello and Iago as a kind of traveling vaudeville team, with Othello the "straight man" for Iago's cutting jibes, leaving us not knowing where the act will go, but certainly not to tragedy. But Othello's fit, during which he physically collapses and is under the care *and control* of Iago, reinforces the notion that the two men have had metaphoric intercourse during which Iago is the controlling male and Othello the dominated female. To compensate for this demeaning experience, Othello *must* dominate Desdemona, whose pure innocence will not yield except to violence.

Othello, like *Hamlet* and *King Lear,* is suffused with male distrust of female sexual attraction. The deep distrust is endemic to Iago, who "implants" his sexual misanthropy into Othello in a kind of hidden homosexual act that mirrors, as discussed above, Iago's wild tale of lying with Cassio. Othello's rage at Desdemona's supposed infidelity casts him as a latter-day sonnet poet, reacting to the Dark Lady who eventually entraps and betrays him. In his diseased mental image of Desdemona, this sick dark man mistakenly casts his innocent white wife as the Dark Lady all men should fear and shun. And so he kills her with diseased logic: "Yet she must die, else she'll betray more men" (5.2.6).

Almost as much as her foolhardy defense of Cassio, the sea voyage turned Desdemona's world upside down. In Cyprus, Iago is in control while poor Desdemona is acted upon. She is no longer in civilized Venice but, by her wish, is honeymooning in a military camp with armed soldiers who carouse and get drunk. She must now try to play the part of a general's wife, a role she neither dreamed of back in Venice nor is equipped to play. She acquires a handmaiden, Iago's wife, Emilia, who for one stunning moment inadvertently becomes the villain's accomplice when she gives him the fateful handkerchief. Desdemona becomes entangled in a dispute between her husband and his lieutenant, Cassio, and she has to make her way against the verbal assaults of Cassio's successor, "honest Iago." All events conspire against her. Except for Emilia,

Desdemona is now alone and fatally burdened by her touching loyalty to the Othello she married in her home town, where their relationship was affectionate and mutually reinforcing. Much like Ophelia, she is perhaps too young and certainly unprepared to understand what is really going on, how she is being sucked into a dispute over rank she has no business in, and helpless against Othello's increasing jealousy over that handkerchief, a trifle, a nothing that becomes everything. How symbolic that her marriage would be threatened by a relic from Othello's past, from a sibyl who "in her prophetic fury" predicted the coming end of the world and whose "raw materials," worms and "mummy," symbolized death. After twice dishonestly declaring to his wife, "I will deny thee nothing,"[115] Othello muses:

> Excellent wretch! Perdition catch my soul
> But I do love thee! And when I love thee not
> Chaos is come again. (3.3.90-92)

"Chaos is come *again*," he says. Othello's former life was *all* chaos. Desdemona was not astute enough both

---

[115]. 3.3.76 and 83.

to understand that and to perceive that sailing away from Venice, symbolically separated from her husband over unknown and stormy seas, represented retreat back to chaos for Othello, not progress into a better world.

A witch? I do not think so, but a foolish young woman who somehow decided to venture into the sexual pleasures of marriage with an older, epileptic black man, perhaps about the same age as her father. When Othello was spinning his yarns in Brabantio's drawing room, his host must have viewed him as an exotic raconteur. But the minute Othello eloped with his daughter, Brabantio saw him as a devil, a consort of mountebanks, an inheritor of arts as black as his skin, descended from the same murky region as the gypsy who first fashioned that poisoned handkerchief. His characterization was not far from wrong, and when Emilia sees the murdered body of her sweet mistress, she twice labels him a devil. Emilia also has it right when she labels him "O gull, O dolt/ As ignorant as dirt" (5.2.158-160), and "O thou dull Moor" (5.2.223).

In reviewing a London production in February, 2008, sagacious John Lahr wrote that "Othello's tragedy lies not so much in the obvious externals of racial difference as in an overwhelming sense of his own unworthiness, which lies hidden beneath his heroics…. For all his accomplishments, Othello cannot believe that he is truly lovable to a white woman."[116] Lahr's comment points toward the kind of cultural prejudice Iago used as one of his tools and Othello could not see beyond. Certainly their tragedy stems from an ill-suited couple who, like Romeo and Juliet, found themselves enmeshed in events that moved too fast for them either to understand or to counteract. Out of naïve loyalty to the stranger she has just married, Desdemona *does* turn her back on her father. As Jessica "killed" Shylock, so Desdemona "killed" Brabantio, as Gratiano tells us in 5.2, "Thy match was mortal to him." What did Brabantio die of — a broken heart, or guilt?[117]

116. John Lahr, "Majestic Moor." *The New Yorker*. January 21, 2008, 84.
117. In Othello's opening, when Brabantio says to Roderigo, "My daughter is not for thee" (1.1.97), perhaps what he meant was, "She's not for thee because she's mine." Also, in that first scene, when

Brabantio begins to suspect that Roderigo and Iago are correct about Desdemona's not being home, he remarks, almost to himself: "This accident is not unlike my dream,/ Belief of it oppresses me already" (1.1.140-141). In the "confrontation" scene, Brabantio tells the Duke and other senators that his "particular grief" is more important than any possible state business – to wit, that his daughter is "dead ... to me" (1.3.56-60). When Desdemona enters, Brabantio addresses her as "gentle mistress" (1.3.178), prompting Honigmann's footnote. All of which leads me to speculate that perhaps Desdemona *was* his gentle mistress, thus accounting for Brabantio's grief at losing her (to Othello, Roderigo, or anyone) and for his distress about his dream. Therefore, as a non-virgin Desdemona could not marry a Venetian. But why not marry this older, peripatetic, dark-skinned fellow, who's lame of sight and perhaps also of brain? Perchance he wouldn't care or was not in a position to care, provided he had a yen to marry a young, white, aristocratic woman. There are reasons to believe that their marriage was never consummated, so Othello never discovered that his new, young wife was "despoiled." And, finally, why did Brabantio die? In the grisly final scene, his brother, Gratiano, reveals he died of "pure grief." Here are Gratiano's lines;

> Poor Desdemona. I am glad thy father's dead;
> Thy match was mortal to him, and pure grief
> Shore his old thread in twain. Did he live now
> This sight [Desdemona dead] would make him do a desperate turn,
> Yea, curse his better angel from his side
> And fall to reprobance.   (5.2.202-207)

Do we not hear an echo of Sonnet 144? There, the poet's "better angel is a man right fair," the poet's special friend. Who is Brabantio's "better angel," Desdemona, or the memory of Desdemona, before she eloped? And his "old thread," cut in two? The thread of life, or the thread of memory of his days (and nights) with Desdemona? Sonnet 144 tells a tale of sexual corruption. Was Brabantio's "pure grief" bred of fear that Othello, when he discovered that his wife was not a virgin, would return to Venice and either try to kill him or reveal to the world his dark secret?

How natural that it is always Desdemona who captures our sympathy, much like Cordelia. Both are loyal and loving to the end. Lear – finally – understood the essence of his daughter's love. Othello cannot rise above his jealousy to see how beautiful Desdemona is, inwardly and outwardly. About six years later, Shakespeare will pen another tale of male jealousy and stupidity, yet he "is still a long way from the mythic view which reimagines Desdemona as Hermione and sets her at the redemptive center of the tragicomic *Winter's Tale.*"[118] As for the ill-fortuned couple in this play, a January and May tale turned sadly sour, at the end their marriage was finally consummated -- grievously on the conjugal death-bed. And just like Juliet, Desdemona never had a chance.

■ *King Lear*

As flies to wanton boys are we to the gods,
They kill us for their sport.

Winter's not gone yet, if the wild geese fly that way.

---

118. Fiedler, 145.

In a recent interview, Sir Ian McKellen, in New York to impersonate Lear, commented that "Your kingship is created entirely by the way other people react to you."[119] The motives, actions, and fates of Lear's three daughters are inextricably woven into the fabric of what Lear does and says in Act One, Scene One, and how his daughters react to him. This monumental drama, thrust between *Hamlet* and *Macbeth*, is the generic blueprint of the father-daughter puzzle, the *alpha* and *omega* of possibilities and outcomes. In the opening scene, Lear fractures family and kingdom, violating the natural order of the universe and liberating those forces that will either restore order or take the rupture to its inevitable, chaotic end. Metaphorically, Lear pries open the lid of Pandora's box, releasing all of mankind's evils. Gloucester's summary pinpoints the family fissure:

> These late eclipses in the sun and moon portend no good to us. ...The King falls from bias of nature – there's father against child. We have seen the best of our time. (1.2.103-12)

119. From John Lahr's Profile, "He That Plays the King." *The New Yorker* August 27, 2007,50.

"The King falls from bias of nature...." Is that the whole play in seven words? The opening scene gives us valuable insights into several of the major characters – Lear, his three daughters, and Kent. Lear emerges as an imperious tyrant, brooking no dissent from his whims. His first words are a gruff command, "Attend the lords of France and Burgundy, Gloucester." How ironic that the man he thus orders will be his companion on the moor, when Gloucester is blind and Lear is mad, preaching the wisdom of Solomon.[120] With "Which of you shall we say doth love us most," Lear catapults his daughters into a love game no one can win. It's hard to believe Lear is serious, that he's not winking and smiling. A needy egoist, he's deadly serious and "holds all the cards."[121] This blustery king prequels Cleopatra's question, her first words in *Antony and Cleopatra,* written about a year after *King Lear:* "If it be love indeed, tell me how much." She throws the line at Antony with a flirtatious

120. In 4.6, Lear says to Gloucester, "I will preach to thee, mark (ll. 176ff). Bloom points out that Lear's "sermon" comes straight from the Seventh Book of the Book of Solomon. Bloom,477.
121. McKellen in Lahr, 50.

smile. He tosses back the appropriate response, "There's beggary in the love that can be reckoned," precisely what Cordelia should have said. In both plays, this cursed query leads to tragedy.

The responses of Goneril and Regan are rife with obvious flattery and tellingly indict Lear's character for being so easily fooled by his daughters' obsequious game playing. Goneril, the first to respond, informs Lear, with stunning irony, that she loves him, "Dearer than eyesight, space and liberty...," for it is Goneril who urges her brother-in-law, in 3.7, to "Pluck out his [Gloucester's] eyes." Goneril receives from her father the gift of liberty, liberty from her demanding father, as well as space – one-third of England, soon to be one-half. And just as Lear's rash actions beget the forces that will destroy him, so her actions engender the gradual shrinking of her space and suffocation of her liberty.

Regan, next at bat in Lear's grim game, tells him, "I am alone felicitate/ In your dear highness' love." Cordelia, who lacks the "glib and oily art" of her sisters, immediately highlights the illogic of their responses, "Why have my sisters husbands, if they say/ They love you all?/ ... Sure I shall never marry like my sisters/ To love my father all." Lear is too pig-headed to hear what she is saying and hears only what she is not saying. The scene is a reprise of 1.3 of *Othello*, when Desdemona says to her father and the assembled Venetian senators, "My noble father,/ I do perceive here a divided duty." The difference is that Desdemona has her husband at her side, and it is she, not her father, who preempts the argument. To her chagrin, unmarried Cordelia is still subject to her father's choice of husband, and Lear wields that fatherly prerogative selfishly and viciously.

Lear turns his back on his youngest daughter, disclaiming "paternal care ... forever." How much more brutal to Cordelia is Lear than Brabantio was to Desdemona!

Here I disclaim all my paternal care ...
And as a stranger to my heart and me

Hold thee from this[122] for ever. (1.1.114-117)

And to France:

> ... for we
> Have no such daughter, nor shall ever see
> That face of hers again. Therefore, be gone,
> Without our grace, our love, our benison.
> (1.1.264-7)

Why is Lear more savage than Brabantio? Lear is both older and politically more powerful. He is a king and Brabantio but a senator. Dramaturgically, Lear controls the scene and the play; Brabantio remains a background character. Brutality is endemic to Lear. Is Shakespeare telling us that if a father does not engage trustfully with his daughter when he is younger, he cannot when he is older, or when he is politically at the zenith? If so, did he change his mind six years later with Prospero? In high dudgeon, little does the furious Lear know how crucial to his life Cordelia's love and paternal care will become when he is carried, like a wounded animal, in a litter to

---

122. Presumably he holds his hand on his heart and gestures toward the room that symbolizes both his court and his family.

Dover. His fury in Act One metamorphoses into *hysterica passio* in Act Two and full-fledged madness in Act Three.

Lear's "gifts" to his daughters are forever gifts. The bounds he gives to Goneril and Albany are theirs and their issues' "perpetual." Regan and Cornwall's "ample third" are "to thee and thine hereditary ever." To Cordelia, he is a stranger "forever." Only after enduring madness and the untamable violence of the elements will Lear learn that Cordelia's love is also a forever gift.[123]

In banishing Cordelia, he invokes the "mysteries of Hecate," as though somehow Cordelia is connected to witches and witchcraft. In truth, only Lear is somehow inspired by witchcraft, not Cordelia, and Lear has no Iago to egg him down this ruinous path. Lear's Iago is his own untamed, self-centered, arrogant nature. Indeed, Kent

---

123. Twice during Lear's journey to madness he alludes to Cordelia, as though some small part of his conscience acknowledges his cruel mistake. The first, and most obvious, in conversation with his Fool before they leave Goneril's palace for Regan's: "I did her wrong" (1.5.24). The second when Regan attempts to convince Lear to return to her sister's: "Return to her? ...Why, the hot-blooded France, that dowerless took/ Our youngest born..." (2.2.396-402).

justifies his bluntness to his king: "… be Kent unmannerly/ when Lear is mad." He urges his master to "check/ This hideous rashness." Tellingly, only Kent and Cordelia call Lear "father."[124] That word never comes from Goneril or Regan until Lear has exited, and they begin to plot against him, "let us hit together." As Lear and his reduced train leave Gloucester's castle and head into the storm, Regan's description is indeed cold-blooded: "This house is little; *the old man* and's people/ Cannot be well bestowed" (2.2.477-478, italics mine). For his candor, the faithful Kent is banished, given five days to leave the kingdom on pain of death. His expulsion echoes Lear's giving away his one true daughter dowryless, even implying some "unchaste action or dishonoured step." And thus Kent and Cordelia are twinned, both unerringly faithful to Lear, one in England, the other in France. Kent is also paired with Edgar, both of whom must don disguises in order to stay faithful to their fathers. As this fateful episode is ending, Kent provides its fitting coda: "Freedom lives hence and

124. Later, the Fool will affectionately call Lear "nuncle."

banishment is here." Unlike hapless Romeo, Kent manipulated his banishment so as to void its power.

Cordelia is so different from her sisters that one wonders if her mother is the same as theirs. In Act Four, Kent ponders the same question. When speaking to a gentleman who delivered Kent's summarizing letter to Cordelia and hearing of Cordelia's reaction to her sisters' cruelty, he wonders how the same progenitors could produce such different daughters:

> It is the stars,
> The stars above us govern our conditions,
> Else one self mate and make could not beget
> Such different issues. (4.3.33-6)

Is it possible that Cordelia is the child of an out-of-wedlock liaison, having come "something saucily to the world," and thus the female echo in Lear's family of Edmund in Gloucester's? If so, the two are paired in absolute contrast with the added irony of Edmund's being the culprit who orders his "twin's" hanging.[125] Or

---

125. 'Tis a wild and wooly notion, I know. But in Lear's first outburst against Goneril, he brands her a "degenerate bastard" (1.4.245), adding

perhaps Goneril and Regan's mother had died and Lear had remarried, adding a kind of Cinderella patina to the relationship of the three sisters.

But what about Goneril and Regan, who occupy so much stage time and are so integral to the movement of the plot? Can we excuse the cruelty of Cordelia's older sisters in light of living with such an imperious and egotistical father? Are Goneril and Regan underground heroines of *King Lear*? Well, in a way, yes. We have no direct evidence of what Goneril and Regan were like as young girls, of how they were brought up, or of the influence of their mother, if she was alive during their formative years. We also know nothing about their choice of husbands and the extent to which each of them entered marriage willingly or had their husbands chosen by their imperious father. Judging from Lear's actions as the play begins, he was harsh and demanding.

---

some small sense of conviction to the idea that Lear's family contained a bastard. In Lear's famous "Let copulation thrive" speech, he comments that "Gloucester's bastard son was kinder to his father/ Than were my daughters got 'tween the lawful sheets" (4.6.113-114). That statement clearly refers only to Goneril and Regan, not to Cordelia.

When Lear asks willfully, "Which of you shall we say doth love us most," the two older daughters may very well have mumbled something like, "Oh, Lord, here we go again," winked at each other, and launched into their encomiums purely to play the game they knew their father desired, that and nothing more. If so, their turning against their father was intentional and bred of some deep dislike.

Much of 1.4 is devoted to Lear's quarrel with his eldest daughter, culminating in Lear's vitriolic denunciation of Goneril:

> Hear, Nature, hear, dear goddess, hear:
> Suspend thy purpose if thou didst intend
> To make this creature fruitful.
> Into her womb convey sterility,
> Dry up in her the organs of increase,
> And from her derogate body never spring
> A babe to honour her.
>   ... that she may feel
> How sharper than a serpent's tooth it is
> To have a thankless child. (1.4.267-81)

Not only does he curse his potential grandchildren but, more generically, he subverts woman's unique power and *raison d'etre,* the creation of new life. On the heath, quite mad and crowned with wild flowers, in his famous "Let copulation thrive" speech, Lear extends his misogynistic venom to subsume all women:

> Down from the waist they are centaurs, though women all above. But to the girdle do the gods inherit, beneath is all the fiend's: there's hell, there's darkness, there is the sulphurous pit, burning, scalding, stench, consumption! Fie, fie, fie! (4.6.121-125)

In 2.2, Lear discovers that Regan is as cold-hearted as her sister, confronts both of them before Gloucester's castle, and then ventures into the stormy night. During this scene, Regan tells Lear:

> O, sir, you are old:
> Nature in you stands on the very verge
> Of her confine. You should be ruled and led
> By some discretion that discerns your state
> Better than you yourself. (2.2.334-39)

And when Lear, desperate to find some charity in Regan, reminds her, "I gave you all," she retorts, "And in good time you gave it" (2.2.439), laying bare her mercenary nature, for all to see.

So Lear's eldest daughters tell their father overtly exactly what the bastard Edmund told himself covertly as he plotted to deceive his father and rid the family of Edgar to obtain Edgar's inheritance for himself: Jacob and Esau played out on the Jacobean stage. Since Goneril and Regan now think alike with Edmund, no wonder they both vie for his affection: birds of a feather.

At the end of Act Two, still before Gloucester's castle, as "the high winds/ Do sorely ruffle," Goneril and Regan abandon their father, a reprise of Joan of Arc's similar denial of hers. As Gloucester entreats them to have pity on the old man, Goneril commands, "My lord, entreat him by no means to stay." And Regan:

> O sir, to willful men
> The injuries that they themselves procure
> Must be their schoolmasters. Shut up your doors.
> (2.2.489-94)

This scene is the cruel echo of "willful" Lear's brutal rejection of Cordelia in 1.1. She will see her father once more before they die; Goneril and Regan will not. When they shut the doors of Gloucester's castle, they shut their own doors on ever seeing their father again. We tend to think of them as mistreating their father, and indeed they do; in fact amidst the storm Gloucester declares, "His daughters seek his death" (3.4.159). But underlying these long scenes of confrontation, first with Goneril, then with Regan, and then with both, is an irony intrinsic to the drama's overplot. Regan's last words, spoken to Gloucester but perhaps within earshot of Lear, reveal what none of the principals yet perceive: "The injuries that they themselves procure/ Must be their schoolmasters."

In Lear's first altercation with Goneril, shortly after the Fool has told his master that little was left except "Lear's shadow," the king promises Goneril that he will, like Proteus, assume his former status:

Thou shalt find
That I'll resume the shape which thou dost think

197

I have cast off forever. (1.4.300-02)

But Lear is wrong. On the moor, clearly not in his proper
mind, he responds to Gloucester's "Is't not the King?"
with "Ay, every inch a king" (4.6.106). But he will never
be able to reassume his kingship. His injuries *will*
become his schoolmaster, and they will teach him, "I
have ta'en/ Too little care" of the "poor naked
wretches" of his kingdom (3.4.33-34, 29), one of whom,
"unaccommodated man," just then magically emerges
from the muck and straw of the hovel. Edgar, Lear's
godson disguised as Poor Tom, becomes Lear's
"philosopher" to help Lear begin to understand the
defining journey of his old age. Pushed to self-
knowledge by Goneril and Regan's cruelty, the king will
learn to become a man.[126] Like the ghost in *Hamlet,*

---

126. Once he becomes homeless, Lear tries to think of himself as the
king, but, like a two-part fugue, he also begins to recognize himself as
generic "man." The first instance occurs when he is addressing the
storm, "I am a man/ More sinned against than sinning" (3.2.59-60).
Climactically, in his recognition scene with Cordelia, twice he identifies
himself as a man: "Pray do not mock me./ I am a very foolish, fond old
man/ …. Do not laugh at me,/ For, as I am a man, I think this lady/ To be
my child Cordelia" (4.7.59-70).

Lear's degenerate daughters are the *force majeure* of *King Lear*.

In *Hamlet,* we have a daughter whose personal desire is compromised by her politically avaricious father; in *Othello* a daughter who abandons her father's household; in *King Lear*, a daughter who is driven away by her father. All three fathers then abandon their natural paternal roles. And so, at the height of his dramatic career, Shakespeare took the pattern we found with Joan in *1 Henry VI*, expanded it, and gave it a central role in three of his most famous tragedies. All five daughters die. Has Shakespeare established some dramatic rule that when a daughter and a father do not attain mutual trust, death cannot be avoided? And are any of the daughters witches, like Joan?

Clearly Goneril and Regan are. When Albany comes to his senses in 4.2, he calls the two "Tigers, not daughters." And a few lines later, to Goneril, his wife, "thou art a fiend,/ A woman's shape doth shield thee" (4.2.41, 67-68). Harking back to Fiedler's observation, quoted in my Introduction, can we say that Cordelia is also subsumed among daughters who turn their backs on their fathers? Fiedler said that they are therefore witches and must die. Well, Cordelia is a witch-doctor, a shaman who can summon the earth's fertility for its healing herbs. In 4.4, when consulting with a "gentleman" (a doctor?) about what care to give her father, she invokes "All you unpublished virtues of the earth" to "spring with my tears. Be aidant and remediate/ In the good man's distress" (4.4.16-18). And when her father has been brought to her side:

> O you kind gods!
> Cure this great breach in his abused nature;
> Th' untuned and jarring senses, O, wind up
> Of this child-changed father. (4.7.14-17)

Cordelia is, indeed, the avatar of long-suffering, patient, paternal love. But Shakespeare casts Cordelia as more than that, as a Christ-like figure who apostrophizes, "O dear father,/ It is thy business that I go about" (4.4.23-24). With the music the doctor commands, Cordelia seeks her father's, the king's, rebirth, much as Paulina conjures music to effect Hermione's restoration. But deep within her care and love is an irony not unlike that buried within her sisters' cruel actions. Returning from France to see her father, she brings an army to restore his kingship when he least wants it.[127] Now he desires only to spend time with his beloved daughter, even if in prison, where

> We two alone will sing like birds i' the cage.
> When thou dost ask me blessing I'll kneel down
> And ask of thee forgiveness. So we'll live
> And pray, and sing, and tell old tales ...
> As if we were God's spies. (5.3.9-17)

Without his daughters, both the evil ones and the kind one, Lear would have been bogged down in "the gored state" of Act One, Scene One. And what does this mean about the role of daughters? Must they always obey their fathers in order to avoid tragedy, even if the fathers are foolish or worse? Until we come to *The Tempest*, most of Shakespeare's daughters had to

---

127. R.A. Foakes has a splendid discussion of this and related points in his Introduction to the *Arden King Lear*. London, Thomson Learning (2007), 20-23.

discover wisdom within themselves or with the help of a confidante in order to assert love and trust in the family and repair the damage foolish, feckless, or phantasmagorical fathers fostered.

■ *Macbeth*

> Now o'er the one half-world
> Nature seems dead, and wicked dreams abuse
> The curtain'd sleep … and wither'd Murther …
> Moves like a ghost.

With *Macbeth* we have perhaps the perfect example of Fiedler's summary comment, quoted in the Introduction, that "There is scarcely a play in the canon in which daughters do not betray or seem to betray their fathers." Not only does Lady Macbeth betray her father, she wants to kill him. In 2.2 she comes perilously close. Fiedler also posited that daughters who disavow their fathers are, *ipso facto,* witches and must die. When Lady Macbeth invokes her evil Spirits to "unsex me here," does her speech signify that she is the real witch of this shortest of Shakespeare's tragedies, a drama so bewitched and with a history so rife with unnatural accidents that thespians dare not even whisper its name but instead use its *nom de plume*, "The Scottish Play"? Absolutely, and not only that, at last we come to a play not just about witches but one that actually contains witches, right there on the stage, before our very eyes. Banquo doesn't know what to make of them:

> What are these,
> So wither'd and so wild in their attire,
> That look not like th'inhabitants o' th'earth
> And are on it? Live you? ... you should be women,
> And yet your beards forbid me to interpret
> That you are so. (1.3.39-47)

While Banquo questions the nature of these numinous creatures, including their gender and even whether they live on this earth, his noble partner is "rapt withal." As Charles Lamb wrote, "From the moment that their eyes first met, Macbeth is spellbound. That meeting sways his destiny. He can never break the fascination."[128] When he writes to Lady Macbeth about this encounter, in his very first sentence he tells her that "I have learn'd by the

---

128. From page 55 of Charles Lamb's Miscellaneous Prose, quoted in Muir's Introduction to *The Arden Shakespeare Macbeth*, xxxv.

perfect'st report, they have more in them than mortal knowledge." Where has he so learned, and by "the perfect'st report?" Whom did he consult? The Devil? Perhaps, but one thing is clear, he has enlisted in the Weird Sisters' army of salvation, and a Faustian bargain seems lurking.

In 3.5, upon the heath, the Sisters and their boss, Hecate, the goddess of the underworld, enact a choric dance to prepare for Macbeth's next encounter. Succinctly, they tell us:

> He shall spurn fate, scorn death, and bear
> His hopes 'bove wisdom, grace, and fear....
> (3.5.30-1)

Their next meeting place tells us who they are: "get you gone,/ And at the pit of Acheron/ Meet me i' th' morning...." In Homer, Acheron is a river of Hades, over which the newly dead are ferried by Charon in order to enter the underworld. So the witches are devils incarnate, dressed as weird women to lure Macbeth to cross over Scotland's flowing Acheron, and he shall "spurn fate [and] scorn death...." The red flag has been raised.

But was Lady Macbeth also cozened? At the end of her husband's letter, his words bait the hook: "This have I thought good to deliver thee (my dearest partner of greatness) that thou might'st not lose the dues of rejoicing, by being ignorant of what greatness is promised thee." She has to read only "what greatness is promised thee" to see herself as Queen of Scotland and experience a chilling frisson.

As we watch this play unfold, we can see three Lady Macbeths, just as there are three weird sisters. After reading Macbeth's letter, in 1.5, and then expressing doubts about her husband's resoluteness, "too full o' th' milk of human kindness," she screws her courage to the sticking-place and resolves not only to feed his vaulting ambition but also to stage-manage their great enterprise:

He that's coming
Must be provided for; and you shall put
This night's great business into my dispatch....

Only look up clear;
To alter favour ever is to fear.
Leave all the rest to me. (1.5.66-73)

As she "stage-manages" their "great business," we come to realize that Shakespeare did not leave Joan of Arc (as witch) behind. She has reappeared here, as Lady Macbeth, in all her hellish splendor. As Fiedler notes, "Lady Macbeth functions not just as another witch, but as the sole substantial reality behind the shadow play of stage convention, hallucination, and delusion represented by the weird sisters...."[129] She is, then, the flesh-and-blood, in-the-action witch, married to Macbeth and devoted to carrying out the hints and guesses of her "other selves," the witches. Fiedler also points out that she and the witches never appear on stage together so that in Shakespeare's day she could literally have been both herself and one of the witches. In so doing, she is the second Lady Macbeth who very soon merges with the stage-manager first.

But in the sleepwalking scene (5.1), a doctor and a

---

129. Fiedler, 72.

maid watch this steely woman of firm resolve disintegrate. Like a young child afraid of the dark, she must have "light by her continually" in her vain attempt to erase the darkness of her deeds. She rehearses Duncan's, Banquo's, and Lady Macduff's murders, and try as she might, she cannot purge her hands of the smell of blood: "Here's the smell of blood still: all the perfumes of Arabia will not sweeten this little hand. Oh! oh! oh!" Sensing the cause of Lady Macbeth's distress, the doctor draws his insightful conclusion: "More needs she the divine than the physician."

So what happened to the first Lady Macbeth to bring about the third? In her concern to become Queen, she decides to play an active role in planning and executing the assassination. First, she'll reprise Claudius and "pour mine spirits into thine ear," which, like a mainline injection of super-charged testosterone, will dissipate "all that impedes [her husband] from the golden round."

But then she takes one fateful step further and invokes certain Spirits for a metamorphosis:

> Come, you Spirits
> That tend on mortal thoughts, unsex me here,

and what kind of Spirits are these?

> And fill me, from the crown to the toe, top-full
> Of direst cruelty! Make thick my blood,
> Stop up th'access and passage to remorse ….
> Come to my woman's breasts,
> And take my milk for gall, you murth'ring ministers….
> (1.5.40-48)

And where did these Spirits come from? Perhaps from France, via Joan *la Pucelle*:

> Now help, ye charming spells and periapts ….
> You speedy helpers, that are substitutes
> Under the lordly monarch of the north,
> Appear and aid me in this enterprise.
> (1 Henry VI, 5.3.2-7)

In case we had any doubt, Joan identifies her "Fiends" as the Devil's surrogates. Or perhaps Lady Macbeth's invocation of the powers of darkness sprang full-blown from Lear's curse on Goneril:

> Hear, Nature, hear, dear goddess, hear:
> Suspend thy purpose if thou didst intend
> To make this creature fruitful.

Into her womb convey sterility,
Dry up in her the organs of increase,
And from her derogate body never spring

A babe to honor her. If she must teem,
Create her a child of spleen, that it may live
And be a thwart disnatured torment to her.
                              (King Lear,1.4.267-275)

Both Lear and–yes–Lady Macbeth struggle with an

innate fear of feminine sexuality. Lear curses his own

unborn grandchildren. In a remarkably similar

incantation, Lady Macbeth asks the darker powers to

Unsex me here,
And fill me, from the crown to the toe, top-full
Of direst cruelty! Make thick my blood.
Stop us th'access and passage to remorse....
                              (1.5.41-4)

Like Goneril, then, who also wished to be cross-

gendered[130] and who also was a witch, Lady Macbeth

wants to assume the manliness she accuses her husband

of lacking. In so doing, she negates woman's primary

---

130. As the battle with Cordelia's French forces begins to build, Goneril, distrustful of her husband's military prowess, says to Edmund, "I must change names at home and give the distaff/ Into my husband's hands" (4.2.17-18).

natural role of childbearing, a mirror of Macbeth's attempts to murder entire family groups – Duncan's, Banquo's, and Macduff's. No wonder she could declare, in the drama's most horrifying speech:

> I have given suck, and know
> How tender 'tis to love the babe that milks me:
> I would, while it was smiling in my face,
> Have pluck'd my nipple from his boneless gums,
> And dash'd the brains out, had I so sworn
> As you have done to this.[131]   (1.7.54-59)

In a stunning episode that concludes 1.6, Duncan enters Inverness, the Macbeths's castle that will become his tomb. With terrifying irony, he declares to Banquo:

> This castle hath a pleasant seat; the air
> Nimbly and sweetly recommends itself
> *Unto our gentle senses.* (1.6.1-3)

He is conversing with Banquo at the threshold of Macbeth's castle, the very place where Hecate holds her

---

131. Kenneth Muir, editor of *The Arden Shakespeare Macbeth*, comments that the passage need not infer that Lady Macbeth had a child by a first husband but only that she compares their resolve to a woman's strongest emotion: 1.7.54-59 fn. Note that she concludes her declaration with a line of perfect iambic pentameter: "had I so sworn as you have done to this."

hellish haunts.[132] In a play where "fair is foul," we should not be surprised that the air seems nimble and sweet.

In the prior scene, as they discuss Duncan's approach, Lady Macbeth had tried to tell her partner that he could not hide his evil ambition: "Your face, my Thane, is as a book, where men/ May read strange matters" (1.5.62-63). The book is the Good Book, and three lines later Lady Macbeth completes the reference to Jesus: "He that's coming/ Must be provided for...." The meek and virtuous Duncan, whom Macbeth recognizes consorts with angels[133] and whose body Macduff calls "The Lord's anointed Temple," greets Lady Macbeth as "our honour'd hostess" by honoring her, Jesus-like, with a mini-parable:

Herein I teach you,
How you shall bid God 'ild us for your pains,
And thank us for your trouble. (1.6.12-14)

Duncan's last words in the drama begin with a special Shakespearian symbol of love and end with a kiss:

---

132. See Anthony DiMatteo, "'Antiqui dicunt': classical aspects of the witches in 'Macbeth.'" *Notes and Queries.* 41.1 (March, 1944).
133. See 1.7.16-20.

Give me your hand[134];
Conduct me to mine host: we love him highly,
And shall continue our graces towards him.
By your leave, hostess. (1.6.28-31)

This gracious king has asked her to lead him to his executioner and then kisses his murderess as his last gesture. It is an inversion of Matthew 26:49, where the guilty one kisses the innocent: "And forthwith he [Judas] came to Jesus, and said, God save thee, Master, and kissed him." Perhaps Judas was luckier than Lady Macbeth. Within the same hour and before Jesus died, he confessed to the Priests, "I have sinned, betraying the innocent blood… [and] he departed, and went, and hanged himself." No such simple and quick resolution for Lady Macbeth as Judas.

She was both unsexed and, in the process, sank deeper into the witches' cauldron. And, as if that weren't trouble enough, she has a father problem, thus joining the long line of female characters who are

---

134. In *King Lear*, as Edgar is leading his blind father to safety and to reconciliation, he repeats this phrase seven times, each time with more love than the previous time.

similarly burdened: Joan of Arc, Juliet, Hermia, Jessica, Ophelia, Desdemona, Goneril, Regan, and Cordelia. But Lady Macbeth's enigma is wholly different. Although Goneril and Regan wish their father dead, they lacked the brio to wield the knife themselves. Lady Macbeth, in her chamber of horrors, comes close:

> I laid their daggers ready;
> He could not miss 'em. – Had he not resembled
> My father as he slept, I had done't. (2.2.11-13)

It's the first crack in her steely resolve and reflects some disturbing memory of life at home, before she married. Macbeth inadvertently carries the blood-stained daggers downstairs and refuses to return to the scene of the crime: "I'll go no more:/ I am afraid to think what I have done;/ Look on't again I dare not." Her response is swift and strong:

> Infirm of purpose!
> Give me the daggers. The sleeping, and the dead,
> Are but as pictures ....
> I'll gild the faces of the grooms withal,
> For it must seem their guilt. (2.2.51-6)

Gilding the grooms is foolish strategy. What motive would they have?[135] Just as foolish as her thinking "A little water clears us of this deed:/ How easy is it then" (2.2.66-67)! Is she just too young, too inexperienced to have thought through the consequences of her actions? Cymbeline's Queen she is not. Despite her gasconade, neither she nor her husband is an accomplished murderer but rather criminals *manqués.*

Act Three opens with Lady Macbeth entering as Queen of Scotland. She now has what she wants but is powerless to stop the killing spree and is beginning to come undone. Act Three, Scene Two, opens this way:

Lady Macbeth: Is Banquo gone from court?

Servant: Ay, Madam, but returns again
                                    to-night.

It's an echo of 1.5:

Macbeth: My dearest love,
                 Duncan comes here to-night.

Lady Macbeth: And when goes hence?

---

135. As Rosse commented to Macduff, "What good could they pretend" (2.4.24)?

| *Macbeth:* | To-morrow, as he purposes. |

| *Lady Macbeth:* | O! never |
| | *Shall sun that morrow see!* |

That was the old callous Lady Macbeth. But this time:

Nought's had, all's spent,
Where our desire is got without content:
'Tis safer to be that which we destroy,
Than by destruction dwell in doubtful joy. (3.2.4-7)

She has slipped and will soon dwell with Macbeth "In the affliction of these terrible dreams,/ That shake us nightly." She manages to get through the great banquet scene with Banquo's revenant twice materializing. Once more, she accuses her husband of being "quite unmann'd," but as the guests leave, she tells him, with the greatest irony, "You lack the season of all natures, sleep." He, with equal irony, responds, "Come, we'll to sleep." Those are her last sane words, her final utterance before her sleep-walking scene.

Macbeth, a true military hero, can slug it out, dying like a man. Why does she come apart at the seams? From the moment she reads Macbeth's letter, detailing his meeting with "these Weird Sisters," she also accepts these misshapen females as her guides, describes them as "fate and metaphysical aid," and swallows whole their entire *gestalt* of equivocation, deceit, and treachery. In her invocation to the Spirits (always a capital "S") that can unsex her, she journeys to their hellish underground, even rehearsing the deed herself:

> Come, thick Night,
> And pall thee in the dunnest smoke of Hell,
> That my keen knife see not the wound it makes,
> Nor Heaven peep through the blanket of the dark,
> To cry, 'Hold, hold!' (1.5.50-4)

So she is in as deep as Macbeth. In fact, Macbeth has taken her father's place, and the only time she calls him "My husband" is immediately after her apostrophe about Duncan's resemblance to her father:

> Had he not resembled
> My father as he slept, I had done't. --- My husband!
> (2.2.12-13)

You can read those lines any way you like, but the

juxtaposition is no accident. Macbeth, her new father and now her leader, reversing the earlier order, can neither save her nor lead her to the light she so desperately searches for when she sleepwalks (5.1.). Both have sold their souls to the witches, the Devil's surrogates, in exchange for the golden round, just as Joan offered to do, imploring her Fiends for help in a battle the French are rapidly losing:

> Cannot my body nor blood-sacrifice
> Entreat you to your wonted furtherance?
> Then take my soul; my body, soul, and all,
> Before that England give the French the foil.
>
> (1 Henry VI, 5.3.20-3)

For Joan, the end-game was a blazing stake. Having sent his ministers, the Weird Sisters, to initiate Macbeth's temptation, the Devil himself now enters. He comes to complete his Faustian contract with the Macbeths.

In 5.3 Seyton (read "Satan")[136] appears as

---

136. In a footnote to 5.3.29, Muir says that "Seyton" is French for "The Setons of Touch, ... hereditary armour-bearers to the Kings of Scotland." Muir also notes that one unnamed critic "wildly" suggests "Seyton" is a "quibble on Satan." My own reading suggests that the wild, unnamed critic was right on target.

Macbeth's adjutant, but not before Macbeth has to summon him three times, once for each Weird Sister. When Macbeth asks for his armour, Seyton replies with devilish intelligence: "'Tis not needed yet." Meanwhile, Lady Macbeth, delirious and desperate for sleep, remains offstage, from whence a plangent sound is heard. Seyton instinctively knows "It is the cry of women, my good Lord," and then leaves Macbeth's war-room to push poor Lady Macbeth over the edge, offstage. With not a little *schadenfreude,* Seyton returns and dryly announces, "The Queen, my Lord, is dead." To which Macbeth, equally dryly, says, "She should have died hereafter...." Who really knows what this anguished line means? This strong woman got sucked into the vortex and soon was way over her head in all that is evil in the nature of mankind. Unlike poor Ophelia, who was driven over the edge by exogenous forces, Lady Macbeth was herself the principal actress in her own demise.

Except for Seyton, his hangman confederate, Macbeth is truly alone now, a kind of anchorite surrounded by rebellious thanes in the dystopian

Scotland his evil schemes have created. Unlike Hamlet, or even Othello, no one will speak for Macbeth. The drama's finale could be Shakespeare's version of Aeschylus's *Seven Against Thebes,* in which King Eteokles ignores the chorus's warning about mutual fratricide, valuing *kerdos* (selfish gain) above everything, even the desire for life.[137] In *Macbeth,* is there any chorus to warn the Thane of Glamis? Actually, yes. Hear now the chorus's words:

This supernatural soliciting
Cannot be ill; cannot be good ....

But in these cases,
We still have judgment here; that we but teach
Bloody instructions, which, being taught, return
To plague th' inventor....
He's here in double trust:
First, as I am his kinsman and his subject,
Strong both against the deed; then, as his host,
Who should against the murtherer shut the door,
Not bear the knife myself.[138]

---

137. This comparison was suggested by a version of the Presidential Address to the Classical Association, given in Glasgow, early in 2009. See the June 19, 2009, issue of *The Times Literary Supplement,* 14-15.
138. An echo of Gloucester, bemoaning to Cornwall and Regan, and reminding them, "You are my guests" (*King Lear,* 3.7.30).

> Besides, this Duncan
> Hath borne his faculties so meek, hath been
> So clear in his great office, that his virtues
> Will plead like angels....
> We will proceed no further in this business:
> He hath honour'd me of late; and I have bought
> Golden opinions from all sorts of people....

The words are Macbeth's. No one sees right from wrong so clearly as he, like Claudius. By the end of the first act, with his ambition pricked by his ambitious wife, he boards up his conscience, but through that closed door march the witches and, finally, "the lordly monarch of the north."[139] Not long after "Great Birnam wood to high Dunsinane hill" comes, Seyton sends his captive out to battle the man not born of woman, *mano a mano,* a fight his *aide de camp* knows Macbeth cannot win. And so the royal couple, tyrants to their countrymen and slaves to their ambition (their *kerdos),* having forfeited their "eternal jewels," discover their end-paths are but "the way to dusty death ... [in] a tale/ Told by an idiot, full of sound and fury,/ Signifying nothing."

---

139. Joan of Arc's sobriquet for Satan in 5.3.6.

❖

INTRODUCTION TO CHAPTER V

The destruction of personal love and trust, so key to the tragedies, especially *Hamlet, Othello*, and *King Lear*, became for Shakespeare the imperative for turning to dramas of reconstructive actions among family members. Scholars call such dramas the "late romances," and reconstituting love and trust is key to all of them. Their central conflict "resides in the experience of a noble, basically good, fatherly man who in some way brings great suffering on himself and those most closely related to him, but who is restored to dignity and power."[140] Without this kind of renewal, I imagine Shakespeare faced going to his grave a sad and perhaps even embittered old man.

Near the end of *The Winter's Tale*, the holy priestess Paulina produces a play so unlike Hamlet's "The Mousetrap" that all we can do is "stand still" and

---

140, Wheeler, 14.

marvel at her patience, insight, and creativity. Hamlet's "Mousetrap," intended to entrap Claudius, instead signals his uncle that Hamlet himself intends to revenge his father's murder. Paulina's awesome command, "Music, awake her; strike!/ 'Tis time; descend ..." (5.3.98-99), calls forth a spiritual harmony that Hermione always possessed but kept hidden until Leontes purged his self-inflicted jealousy by sixteen years of prayer and contrition, a kind of earthly Purgatory, perhaps not too dissimilar from the ghost of Hamlet's father's abode.

In *The Tempest,* Shakespeare narrows his focus even further. It was as though he said to himself, "Looking back at all the families of my stage, from the Tudors to the Venetians and then to Sicilia and Bohemia, like Leontes, I, too, have purged away previous familial poisons. A father has emerged whose cherubin of a daughter preserves his spirit in that 'rotten carcass of a butt' and who, in return, lavishes all his powers to assure her future. What counts now is the next generation." Prospero's love for his daughter is all-in-all:

> You are so strongly in my purpose bred
> That all the world besides methinks are dead.
>
> (Son 112)

> Love alters not with his brief hours and weeks,
> But bears it out even to the edge of doom.
>
> (Son. 116)

With the possible exception of Lear's love for Cordelia, at the end, is there any paternal love in all of Shakespeare that can match Prospero's?

It was not a Utopian vision, for on Prospero's magic island we meet representatives of all the courtly vices and some of the virtues. But woven between them is someone new, someone androgynous by nature who embodies the heart and soul of Shakespeare's creative genius. It is a sprite, a spirit, something burning deep within him which he calls "Ariel." She can raise tempests, produce banquets, punish conspirators but who, in the end, wants only her freedom, wants to leave her master,[141] never to be seen again.

"I'll Be Seeing You."[142]

CHAPTER V. The Miracle of Rebirth
The Winter's Tale, The Tempest

■ *The Winter's Tale*

It is requir'd
You do awake your faith. Then all stand still:
Or --- those that think it is unlawful business
I am about, let them depart.

In reviewing a recent production of Euripides's *The Bacchae,* Daniel Mendelsohn claimed that "the Greeks saw women as inherently dishonest, prone to tricks and plots."[143] Many years earlier, Franz Kafka told a friend,

---

141. Although by instinct I have always considered Ariel "feminine," until I read the following in Richard Wheeler's great book, I had nothing to support my feeling: "The maternal capacities to give and withhold essential nurture … are incorporated into Prospero's magic, as in the banquet Ariel first provides and then withdraws from the distraught visitors." Wheeler, 219.
142. With apologies to Rodgers and Hart.
143. Daniel Mendelsohn, "A Wild Night in the Park." *The New York Review of Books*, October 27, 2009, 28.

"Women are snares which lie in wait for men on all sides, in order to drag them into the merely finite."[144] "On all sides," said Kafka; so is there no exit? And what of Shakespeare, writing somewhere in between? Are all women like Kafka's "snares," or like Fiedler's "strangers," or like the trap-door of the Dark Lady, or like Lady Macbeth, canoodling her husband's ambition so that at the end he dared fight the man not born of woman?

Around the turn of the century (circa 1602), Shakespeare experimented with the idea that a woman could restore a man to health, and a king at that. The core action in *All's Well That Ends Well* is Helena's ability to cure the king of his "incurable" malady. When she quite magically does so, she rehabilitates his masculine powers and his ability to influence Bertram's actions so that finally Helena gets her man.[145] The vigor and virtue of the king, restored to his full powers by a woman, and

144. Gustav Janouch, *Conversations With Kafka*. New York, New Directions (1971), 178.
145. For a full exposition of this theme in *All's Well*, see Chapter II of Wheeler, 35 ff.

the notion of reciprocal love and trust between a man and a woman, especially between a king and a woman, are more fully played out and invested in *The Winter's Tale.* Forgiveness and reconciliation, then, are part and parcel of the central meaning of what is probably Shakespeare's penultimate solo drama.

Compared with *All's Well,* perhaps a "problem comedy," *A Winter's Tale* is a veritable cornucopia of rich speeches and images, of contraries, converses, opposites and similarities, and of meanings within meanings, written when Shakespeare was at the height of his dramatic power. Interestingly, perhaps even puzzlingly, it begins with a king turned mad, King Lear *in media res.* Polixenes, Leontes's oldest and best friend, his boyhood buddy, is visiting Sicilia, and Leontes fantasizes that Polixenes is having an affair with his queen, Hermione. As if that were not bad enough, he is sure that Polixenes is the father of very pregnant Hermione's unborn child. What a way to begin this show!

Near the very end of *Hamlet,* as Hamlet and Laertes are about to duel for their lives, Claudius drops a poison pellet into a phial of wine. It's his backup plan in case Laertes's unbated and envenomed rapier misses its mark. Claudius calls what he puts in the goblet "an union." Speaking in the impersonal third person, he announces that

> The King shall drink to Hamlet's better breath,
> And in the cup an union shall he throw
> Richer than that which four successive kings
> In Denmark's crown have worn[146] …. (5.2.267-71)

By "better breath" he means non-breath, which is death. The union, or pearl, that Claudius claims is richer than four generations of Denmark's royal family represents just the opposite – the destruction of family values that Claudius initiates by killing his brother, the king, and seducing his wife, the queen. The "union" represents disunion engendered by incest and corruption. In *The Winter's Tale*, the pearl in the chalice becomes the spider "in the cup" that Leontes imagines he drinks, also

---

146. Has Claudius been looting the royal gem collection?

symbolic of sexual degradation and corruption, all self-inflicted.

And how close Leontes comes to destroying his entire family! Despite Hermione's pregnancy, Leontes has clapped her in jail where she delivers a baby girl. When Paulina brings the newborn before the king, which she calls a "copy of the father," Leontes explodes in a rage, calling her a witch, "A callat/ Of boundless tongue …. A gross hag!/ … worthy to be hang'd" (2.3.90-91, 98-99, 107-108), and he orders his lackeys to "commit them [mother and daughter] to the fire." Leontes, himself now in Hell, sees Paulina as a witch. Luckily for her, he did not read Exodus 22:18. In this first half of the play, Paulina represents Leontes's negative *alter ego.* When he says, "Go out," she comes in. When he asks for silence, she rants on, right in his face. She constantly pushes against him and by some magical process escapes being hanged or herself thrown into Leontes's burning, fiery furnace, undoubtedly in the basement of his palace.

In the beginning, they are polar opposites in a play that must embrace opposites in order to create something new and loving. Paulina instinctively understands that Leontes's violent curses come from a man deranged with self-inflicted jealousy. Unlike Lady Macbeth, nowhere does Paulina ask to be "unsexed." She remains true to her feminine calling -- to protect the honor and person of her mistress, Queen Hermione, and in so doing preserve the royal family that Leontes comes close to destroying. Even though he is her King, she refuses to be cowed by Leontes because she knows that with a little luck, she can bring about his restoration along with his queen's – Helena of *All's Well* writ new and shining. When he threatens, "I'll ha' thee burnt" (an echo from *1 Henry VI*), this lady's not for burning:

> I care not:
> It is an heretic that makes the fire,
> Not she which burns in't. I'll not call you tyrant ....

but that is exactly what she calls him:

> But this most cruel usage of your queen ---
> Not able to produce more accusation

Than your weak-hing'd fancy --- something savours
Of tyranny, and will ignoble make you,
Yea, scandalous to the world. (2.3.113-20)

And just before his courtiers convince Leontes not to see the babe "instantly consum'd with fire," he rants, "The bastard brains with these my proper hands/ Shall I dash out" (2.3.139-140). It's King Leontes, not Paulina, as Lady Macbeth, his first gender change. In this part of the drama, he is, in fact, in Hell and is also, like Macbeth, an insomniac: "Nor night, nor day, no rest..." (2.3.1). When you're in Hell, perhaps you're neither male nor female – or perhaps both at once.

However, Paulina is not the victim of his jealousy. Victimized is his own queen, whom he was wont to address as "Hermione, my dearest," until the green-eyed monster swallowed him whole. Then he contracted "*tremor cordis,*" seen and drank the spider, and in public, before his entire court, labeled Hermione an "adultress" and a "bed-swerver." As Paulina warned, he became "scandalous to the world."

Leontes begins every castigation speech by lamenting his own grief. Like Claudius and Macbeth, no one understands and describes his sickness as clearly as he. His diseased imagination, his "weak-hing'd fancy," is offset by Hermione's grace, a word she uses carefully, with religious overtones[147] (see her speech, just below). Her beautiful, measured discourse contrasts sharply with Leontes's abrupt, spasmodic, mad rants, and she, like Paulina, points the finger of accusation exactly where it belongs and correctly prophesizes that Leontes must undergo a period of grief:

> How will this grieve you,
> When you shall come to clearer knowledge, that
> You thus have publish'd me! Gentle my lord
> You scarce can right me thoroughly, then, to say
> You did mistake....
> I must be patient till the heavens look
> With an aspect more favourable. Good my lords ...
> I have
> That honourable grief lodg'd here which burns

---

147. For example (from OED): "The divine influence which operates in men to regenerate and sanctify and to impart strength to endure trial and resist temptation."

Worse than tears drown[148] ....
This action I now go on [i.e., to prison]
Is for my better grace. Adieu, my lord:
I never wish'd to see you sorry; now
I trust I shall. (2.1.96-100; 106-112; 121-24)

In his superb Introduction to the Arden edition, J.H.P. Pafford aptly describes Hermione as "a woman not only of deep virtue but of divine strength in the power of her unconquerable love, which is love for her husband, for her daughter, her friends, and her own honour and good name. Her nature is open and her love is generous."[149] At the close of his career, Hermione is the apotheosis of Shakespeare's interest in the theme of forgiveness and reconciliation. In *The Winter's Tale,* this theme is centered in three women – Paulina, Hermione, and Perdita.

But the plot line revolves not around them but around the two male protagonists, both kings, both deeply flawed. Their failing, like a sickness, can be cured only by the resolute, intelligent, and loving actions of

---

148. A gracious echo of Hamlet's "But I have that within which passeth show,/ These but the trappings and the suits of woe" (1.2.85-86).
149. J.H.P Pafford, ed. *The Arden Shakespeare The Winter's Tale.* London, Thomson Learning (2006), lxviii.

these three women, a necessary precondition to reciprocal love and trust between a man and a woman. Early in the play, Polixenes describes for Hermione his primal years with Leontes, his best friend. "We were," he tells her, "as twinn'd lambs that did frisk i' th' sun" (1.2.67).[150] The idyll he paints from memory is counterpoised by the sheep shearing festival in Act Four, a real idyll the audience can see on stage. The lyric of Polixenes's youth is interrupted and spoiled by Woman, to whose role in the Garden of Eden he alludes:

> We knew not
> The doctrine of ill-doing, nor dream'd
> That any did. Had we pursu'd that life ...
> We should have answered heaven
> Boldly 'not guilty', the imposition clear'd
> Hereditary ours. (1.2.69-74)

This reference is echoed, a little later in the same scene, when Hermione and Polixenes, after commenting on the change in Leontes's mien, exit to walk in the

---

150. The "twinned lambs," like Perdita, become lost and must be recovered. Fittingly, it is Perdita as shepherdess who leads to the lambs' recovery, whereas the old shepherd, as Perdita's putative father, and Polixenes, her future father-in-law, who unwittingly lead to her recovery.

garden: "If you would seek us,/ We are yours i' th' garden" (Hermione to Leontes, ll. 177-178). The innocence and beauty of this early-youth idyll can lead the reader to wonder if what Leontes is angry about is the loss of his childhood friend, now a grown man, with a son of his own, a king running his own show and no longer Leontes's to play with. Many commentators shy away from assigning a cause for Leontes's jealousy – Leontes is simply his egotistical self and Iago all wrapped up in one. Here, for example, is E.M.W. Tillyard:

> "Leontes's obsession of jealousy is terrifying in its intensity. It reminds us not of other Shakespearian errors, but rather of the god-sent lunacies of Greek drama, the lunacies of Ajax and Heracles. It is as scantily motivated as these, and we should refrain from demanding any motive."[151]

---

151. E.M.W. Tillyard, *Shakespeare's Last Plays*. New York, Barnes and Noble (1968), 41.

Tillyard's description of Leontes's jealousy as a god-sent lunacy is quite apt, but Freudians would never accept his reluctance to probe.

Writing in the preeminent journal of psychoanalysis, co-founded by Sigmund Freud in 1939, Murray Schwartz shows no such temerity. When Hermione convinces Polixenes to stay in Sicilia longer, after Leontes could not, and when the two stroll into the garden, perhaps arm in arm, Schwartz posits the cause of Leontes's jealousy to the subconscious loss of a homosexual attachment to his old friend: "Leontes converts the sexual motive of his tie to Polixenes into a perverse relationship between his wife and his friend. Hermione replaces Leontes and, in his fantasy, acts out the prohibited role Leontes repudiates in himself."[152] Schwartz admits that the script itself reveals "only unspecified suggestions of boyhood" behavior, but cites a tantalizingly vague speech by Leontes to Florizel in the last act:

---

152. Murray M. Schwartz, "Leontes' Jealousy in The Winter's Tale." *American Imago* 30.3 (Fall, 1973), 251.

> Were I but twenty-one,
> Your father's image is so hit in you,
> His very air[153], that I should call you brother,
> As I did him, and speak of something wildly
> By us performed before. (5.1.125-29)

We can also wonder (and perhaps grin) at precisely what Polixenes meant when he told Hermione that he and Leontes did *"frisk* I' th' sun." Was it something more than "like young lambs" or like "something wildly by us performed?" This approach is full of fun and games, and were I something more than Freud Lite, I'd myself linger and perhaps frisk a little with hidden meanings. But the major point is that whatever went wrong in Leontes's head, it probably was related to his boyhood adventures with Polixenes that evidently continued beyond their teen-age years. [154]

And just as Leontes's peace and quiet was shattered by what appeared to be his wife's too-forward behavior, so too was Polixenes's world spoiled by a

---

153. A pun on "heir."
154. Schwartz's follow-up article, "The Winter's Tale: Loss and Transformation," is a brilliant elucidation of all the major characters and themes of the play. *American Imago* 32.2 (Summer, 1975), 145-199.

woman, by Perdita, who seems just a shepherd's daughter but who has stolen his son's heart and ruined the patrilineal dream Polixenes has constructed in Bohemia. Perdita trespasses, breaks the rules of Polixenes's Bohemian Garden, just as Hermione appeared too forward in Leontes's Sicilian garden, and just as Eve broke God's rule in Eden. The irony of the counterpoint is that it will be first Leontes, his former friend and now his enemy, who begins to set things aright although in reality three women, Paulina, Hermione, and Perdita give birth to a new and more glorious love-story for these two old friends.

On Prospero's magical island of reality, as his "project" is about to "gather to a head," faithful Gonzalo summarizes what he and we have witnessed:

O, rejoice ... In one voyage
Did Claribel her husband find at Tunis;
And Ferdinand, her brother, found a wife
Where he himself was lost; Prospero his dukedom
In a poor isle; and all of us ourselves,
When no man was his own. (5.1.206-13)

In the sense that *The Winter's Tale* helped Shakespeare prepare for *The Tempest,* "when no man was his own" is *apropos* the two kings, Leontes and Polixenes. So while Woman is at the core of Man's inner problem, only she can provide the path to curative self-knowledge. In this play, without a woman, neither king "was his own" man, was the man he was meant to be. Although Polixenes had a little help from honourable Camillo and his constant (nay, stubborn) son, his path was paved first by Perdita. His instinct gave him a clear message that she was not what she seemed:

> This is the prettiest low-born lass that ever
> Ran on the green-sward: nothing she does or seems
> But smacks of something greater than herself,
> Too noble for this place. (4.4.156-59)

By "Too noble for this place," he snobbishly means the shepherds' peasant festival, but the irony is that she is also too noble for his conventional Bohemian kingdom and pointedly cuts across the class line Polixenes insists exists. As Perdita explains:

> I was about to speak, and tell him plainly,

The selfsame sun[155] that shines upon his court
Hides not his visage from our cottage, but
Looks on alike. (4.4.444-47)

From Perdita, Polixenes's road to be taken wended
back, in the final act, to Hermione: "The very life seems
warm upon her lip" (5.3.66). For Leontes, his path has
been paved, even before he realized it, by Paulina. Near
the play's end, he gives her the power to choose another
wife for him: "My true Paulina,/ We shall not marry till
thou bid'st us" (5.1.81-81). Thus the two exchange
traditional roles: Paulina is the father choosing, and
Leontes the daughter accepting. In Part One, Leontes
was such a wicked ruler and husband that only after
sixteen years of penitence did he learn that substance is
more important than the cosmetics of tradition. But all
of Paulina's intercourse with her king had but one
purpose, to lead him, eventually, back to his reborn
queen.

In the sheep shearing festival, actors sing and
dance *to each other,* not to the audience.[156] Schwartz

---

155. Undoubtedly a pun on "son."

labels this pastoral festival "a resilient defense against the sexual and familial dislocations dramatized earlier," that is, in Leontes's court. "It comprises a full-scale play-within-the-play...."[157] The star of this play is Perdita, whom Tillyard characterizes "the play's main symbol of the powers of creation."[158] Always the realist, she predicts the coming passionate disagreement between Florizel and his father: "... even now I tremble/ To think your father, by some accident/ Should pass this way, as you did..." (4.4.18-20). Like Juliet, she has the ability to see through present events to their near-term implications. But Florizel is unfazed and declares his intention to marry her, no matter what – "To this I am most constant,/ Though destiny say no." He compares the arrival of their visitors to the arrival of their wedding company: "Be merry, gentle.... Your guests are coming:/ Lift up your countenance, as it were the day/ Of

---

156. At a recent meeting of The Shakespeare Society in New York, well known director Sam Mendes told us that this had never been done before in any Shakespeare play. He called it the beginning of musical comedy.
157. Schwartz, 169.
158. Tillyard, 44.

celebration of that nuptial which/ We two have sworn shall come" (4.4.46-51).

The scene contains Florizel's great love-song to his intended, including these lovely lines:

> … when you do dance, I wish you
> A wave o' th' sea, that you might ever do
> Nothing but that, move still, still so,
> And own no other function. (4.4.140-43)

Schwartz fittingly points out that "the lines *create* the rhythm they are about. When we listen to that rhythm do we not hear the motion of the wave? Do we not hear, also, the echo of Leontes' erupting madness, now transformed into its opposite?

> … my heart dances,
> But not for joy – not joy. (1.2.110-11)"[159]

Importantly, Florizel is dressed as Apollo, "the fire-rob'd god." Now Florizel symbolizes personal truth; he serves as the link to the trial-and-Oracle scene in Sicilia, 3.2.132ff, the immediate cause of Leontes's *anagnorisis*

---

159. Schwartz, 170.

(self-recognition) and his pledge to spend the next sixteen years in prayer and penitence. Florizel, the new, young Apollo, brings light and truth to mankind. In this scene, no one is yet himself: Florizel is Doricles, Perdita a shepherd's daughter called Flora,[160] and both Polixenes and Camillo enter disguised. Not until the final scene, directed by Paulina, will each person discover his true self, as Gonzalo promised.[161]

The horticultural debate is also dominated by Perdita.[162] She distributes to Polixenes and Camillo,

---

160. Northrop Frye commented on the virtual fusion of the names Flora and Florizel, symbolizing a continuity in their relationship that Leontes and Hermione did not attain. "Recognition in The Winter's Tale," in *Shakespeare: 'The Winter's Tale': A Casebook*, ed. Kenneth Muir. London (1968), 194.

161. See *The Tempest*, 5.1.206-213.

162. For a more detailed exposition of the horticultural conversations, see Charles R. Forker, "Negotiating the Paradoxes of Art and Nature in The Winter's Tale," *Approaches to Teaching Shakespeare's "The Tempest" and Other Late Romances*, ed. Maurice Hunt (New York, 1992), 94-102; Richard Hillman, "The Gillyvors' Exchange in The Winter's Tale," *English Studies in Canada* I (1979), 16-23; Mary L. Livingston, "The Natural Art of The Winter's Tale," *Modern Language Quarterly* 30 (1969), 340-355; William O. Scott, "Seasons and Flowers in The Winter's Tale," *Shakespeare Quarterly* 14 (1962), 411-417; James H. Sims, "Perdita's 'Flowers O'th'spring' and 'Vernal Flowers' in Lycidas," *Shakespeare Quarterly* 22 (1971), 87-90; and Derek Traversi's chapter on The Winter's Tale in Kenneth Muir, ed. *Shakespeare The Comedies*. Englewood Cliffs: Prentice-Hall: 1965, 157-163.

somewhat to their annoyance, flowers that are suitable to "men of middle age." The scene bears an echo of Ophelia's distribution of flowers to Claudius, Gertrude, and Laertes. Ophelia was slowly descending to the lower depths. Perdita was ascending to a sphere of higher wisdom. To Florizel she gives "daffodils,/ That come before the swallow dares ... violets, dim,/ But sweeter than the lids of Juno's eyes/ Or Cytherea's breath; pale primroses,/ That die unmarried, ere they can behold/ Bright Pheobus in his strength...." And when Florizel playfully asks her whether she is covering his dead body with all her flowers, her response beautifully combines sexual passion with maidenly restraint and ends with an evocation of the Holy Spirit:

> No, like a bank, for love to lie and play on:
> Not like a corpse; or, if --- not to be buried,
> But quick, and in mine arms. Come, take your flowers:
> Methinks I play as I have seen them do
> In Whitsun pastorals[163].... (4.4.118-34)

---

163. Whitsun (or Whitsuntide) celebrates the arrival of the Holy Spirit to bless and convert the celebrants. See Acts 2.

As Schwartz so astutely reminds us, "Perdita encompasses sexual differences (virginal *and* erotic), social differences (shepherdess *and* "queen"), mythic differences (Flora *and* Persephone), and, in imagistic terms, differences in the substances of life itself (earth *and* water)."[164] In this scene, Perdita is another Rosalind, guiding her lover amidst the greensward but going beyond anything Rosalind had available since they are headed for their apotheosis as future king and queen of Bohemia.

The botanical debate between Polixenes and Perdita covers a lovely irony, for each of them speaks with forked tongue. They argue in favor of what they intend *not* to do "in real life." Shakespeare, sitting in the wings, is amused by their mutual hypocrisy and therefore punishes both of them, but not with a heavy hand. Perdita has to suffer the hasty flight to another country where her future is unknown. Polixenes has to suffer when his son flees his kingdom. But this is a romance, and all will be well, Jack will have his Jill.

---

164. Schwartz, 181-182.

During the festival scene, Polixenes's anger at his son mirrors Leontes's at Hermione. Both kings seem obsessed with sexuality, a clear hint that their own sex lives left much to be desired. First Leontes in this conversation with Camillo:

> Is whispering nothing?
> Is leaning cheek to cheek? Is meeting noses?
> Kissing with inside lip?... horsing foot on foot?
> (1.2.284-8)

And as he is about to leave the festival, Polixenes to Perdita:

> If ever henceforth thou
> These rural latches to his entrance open,
> Or hoop his body more with thy embraces ...

concluding his farewell with a threat as brutal as any Leontes issued to his wife and reminiscent of Lear's to his two degenerate daughters[165]:

> I will devise a death as cruel for thee
> As thou art tender to't. (4.4.438-42)

---

165. "I will do such things ---/ What they are yet I know not, but they shall be/ The terrors of the earth" (2.2.469-471)!

After all, as Polixenes had told Hermione, "We were as twinn'd lambs." Both kings are outraged by mistaken assumptions about wife and son. If Polixenes were not an arrogant king, he might have gone along with his son's marriage to "a shepherd's daughter." He saw how beautiful and gracious Perdita was, as well as the happiness of the festival, informed by "the easygoing laughter of regenerative naturalness."[166] But Florizel excluded his father from all the planning. In talking to the "stranger," Florizel made this quite clear. He pushed his father away, just as Leontes pushed his wife and new-born babe away in Part One, and just as Joan pushed her father so violently away in *1 Henry VI*. Both Leontes and Polixenes have some way to go on their journeys before family fractures are ready to be healed.

Florizel's firm and constant love and Camillo's devotion to personal honour as well as his charming homesickness bring the action back to Sicilia. The ritual of healing demands their return. Twice Camillo

---

166. Tom Absher. *Men and the Goddess*: Feminine Archetypes in Western Literature. Rochester, VT, Park Street Press (1990), 6.

abandons his master to pursue what he regards as the more virtuous path. Both times he is correct, and his devotion to the concept of honour is key to both. Sensing that Camillo knows why Leontes has turned a cold shoulder, Polixenes conjures Camillo "by all the parts of man/ Which honour does acknowledge ... that thou declare" what the problem is.

Camillo: Sir, I will tell you;
Since I am charg'd in honour, and by him
That I think honourable. (1.2.406-08)

Camillo, like Hermione, responds to a challenge to honour. The act ends with that tell-tale Shakespearean symbol of honourable love when Polixenes beseeches Camillo, "Give me thy hand,/ Be pilot to me ...," like Dante to Beatrice and, twelve lines later, like Aeneas to Anchises:

Come, Camillo,
I will respect thee as a father if
Thou bear'st my life off. (1.2.447-48; 460-62)

And then, when it comes time to leave Bohemia and rescue the budding romance of Florizel and Perdita from

Polixenes's wrath, once again Camillo depends on Florizel's recognition of his virtuous motive:

> On mine honour,
> I'll point you where you shall have such receiving
> As shall become your highness; where you may
> Enjoy your mistress ....
> Marry her,
> And with my best endeavors in your absence
> Your discontenting father strive to qualify
> And bring him up to liking. (4.4.526-34)

Camillo's defection from Leontes carries a faint echo of Enobarbus's forsaking Antony. In his speech of penitence, just before Paulina announces Hermione's "death," Leontes recognizes how blamelessly "Camillo tardied/ My swift command" and mentions that Camillo "quit his fortunes here/ Which you knew great" (3.2.162-163, 167-168). But Leontes is no Antony and never thought of sending Camillo's fortunes after him to Bohemia. Conversely, Camillo will bring Leontes's fortunes – his daughter, his putative son-in-law, and boyhood friend – back to Leontes, a singular gift over a stormy sea.

How important, then, are sea voyages in Shakespeare! Hamlet must go to sea and fight the pirates before he can recognize, "There is a special providence in the fall of a sparrow." For Desdemona, the voyage to Cyprus changes everything. In both *The Winter's Tale* and *The Tempest* a babe is exposed to mortal danger at sea. In *The Winter's Tale*, Perdita (not yet named) is carried across the sea by Antigonus, perhaps to her death and certainly to his. In order to fulfill her destiny, she *must* re-cross the same sea, back to her homeland and back to the father who almost had her committed to the flames.[167] But this time she is accompanied by faithful Florizel, whose love for her never wavers, despite his father's threats, and this time her own as yet unrecognized father has spent sixteen years in prayer and penitence. Leontes greets them by saying, "Welcome hither,/ As is the spring to th' earth" (5.1.150-151). Florizel and Perdita bring rebirth to Leontes and his kingdom so that even chilly Sicilia is

---

167. Perdita's life journey parallels Shakespeare's: from a small country town in the Midlands to England's great urban center and then back home to the country.

itself transformed into a warm and welcoming kingdom. Everyone except Camillo undergoes metamorphosis. Steadfast Camillo will undergo marriage.

In a December, 2008 performance by The Shakespeare Theater of New Jersey, at this point director Brian Crowe made one small but wonderful change in Shakespeare's script. Just as the young couple is getting acquainted with Leontes and Paulina, with Florizel desperately trying to pass off Perdita as the daughter of "the warlike Smalus" of Libya,[168] a Lord announces Polixenes's arrival, hell-bent on intercepting the couple and threatening both with "divers deaths in death." (He is still in high dudgeon.) They need Leontes's help, and Crowe gave Florizel's speech to Perdita: "Beseech you, sir …/ Step forth mine advocate…" (5.1.217-222). It was a stunning tableau, with unrecognized daughter, on her knees, pleading with unrecognized father for crucial help, second in

---

168. Frye noticed that this means Shakespeare gave Perdita four fathers: "a real one, a putative one who later becomes her father-in-law, a fictional one, Smalus of Libya … and a shepherd foster-father." Frye. 190, quoted in Schwartz, 180.

emotional wallop only to the statue scene. Fortunately, she pleads before a new – yes, reborn – Leontes, and he is quick to respond: "I am friend to them and you: upon which errand/ I now go toward him [Polixenes]: therefore follow me/ And mark what way I make" (5.1.230-232). Not even Florizel's obvious deviousness could prevent *this* Leontes from greeting *this* Polixenes, his old, dear friend.

So does that mean Shakespeare has banished all witches from deep within his memory? It is clear he is still fixated on father/daughter and father/son relationships; family is all-in-all for him. As detailed above (page 179), Paulina enters the drama very much the harridan, scolding Leontes as well as his timid courtiers. For the deranged king, she is, indeed, a "mankind witch." Even heavenly Hermione has some witch buried deep within her.

In 3.3, Antigonus stands alone on the shore of Bohemia, above the thunder of the turbulent sea and about to face the hungry growl of a bear. In the play's longest speech (43 lines), he relates a vision of Hermione, who also stood alone in court to face the roar of her husband. In last night's dream, Hermione appears to him and requests the infant be named Perdita, "for the babe is counted lost forever." In the first part of the dream, Hermione appears like an angel, "in pure white robes." Three times[169] the queen bowed before him, emphasizing her naming request. In the second part, she becomes a witch who tells him he shall be punished for his role in ostracizing the babe by never seeing his wife again. It is as though Hermione, momentarily a witch in control of Nature, conjures the bear to carry out her dire prediction. "And so, with shrieks,/ She melted into air" (3.3.36-37). Is the bear Leontes, at his most violent, conjured by Hermione so that he will not wreak vengeance on her body? Surely Shakespeare means us to ponder every meaning of the word "bear," especially as it pertains to childbirth and to enduring abuse, verbal and otherwise. It seems that even at this late stage in his

---

169. Three is an important number, both in divinity and in witchcraft. I suspect it's also Shakespeare's favorite number.

career, when he creates two holy women, Paulina and Hermione, the image of Woman as witch still remains imbedded somewhere in Shakespeare's literary or dramatic subconscious.

If Woman as witch still captivated Shakespeare, what about the Dark Lady of the Sonnets? Is she buried in his past, gone and forgotten? Well, not quite. Act Two, Scene One begins charmingly with Hermione, her son, Mamillius, and two Ladies in Waiting. In this scene we learn that Hermione is pregnant, and Mamillius gives us the line from which the title is taken: "A sad tale's best for winter." That the line is Mamillius's clearly signals his importance to the drama's meaning.[170] The winter setting tells us the drama will have a seasonal theme, which we can later label "life, death, rebirth." And that Mamillius notices that the Second Lady echoes

---

170. As his father was with Polixenes, Mamillius is "twinned" with Florizel. Paulina tells us that "there was not a full month/ Between their births" (5.1.117-118). In one sense, Mamillius's death reflects Shakespeare's disillusion with the father-son pattern for solving familial and societal dislocations. He left that pattern behind in the histories, especially the Henriad, and moved in the late romances to the father-daughter archetype.

the poet's Dark Lady[171] warns us that trouble lies ahead, perhaps relating to Hermione's unborn child. In much the same manner, Shakespeare has given us a subtle but unmistakable hint that jealousy will rear its green and ugly head when in 2.2 the name of the only one of Hermione's Ladies allowed to accompany her to prison is Emilia, the same as Iago's wife, Desdemona's handmaid and the only one who is close to her in that drama's hideous denouement, a death-prison. Hermione's Emilia tells us that her mistress has delivered a girl; she speaks twenty lines and is heard no more.

So how do Paulina and Hermione as temporary witches advance Shakespeare's dramatic invention? In much the same way that Polixenes's anger at his son mirrors Leontes's at his wife and Florizel's rejection of his father mirrors Leontes's of his wife and newborn. What is broken will be fixed; where faith has been lost, it will be found; forgiveness and reconciliation are now

---

171. When Mamillius tells the Second Lady he loves her more than the First and she asks why, he responds, "Not for because/ Your brows are blacker; yet black brows, they say,/ Become some women best...." Cf. Sonnet 127.

in the very air of Sicilia. Everyone will be transformed from what they were, "dissever'd," in a kind of sleep, to what they should be in Leontes's renewed kingdom. In executing Hermione's metamorphosis, a mystical rebirth that transfigures everyone, Paulina first requires music: "Music, awake her; strike!/ 'Tis time; descend …" (5.3.98-99). She can now command time (i.e., nature) and insist there be no delay, sixteen years or any. It is the first and only time we hear music in Sicilia.[172] Jill Line tells us that "the mythological Hermione is the daughter of Mars and Venus whose other name is Harmonia…." Leontes's accusations and evil actions in Part One created a cacophony of his being, his family, and his kingdom. Now Paulina understands that the moment has come to re-establish musical integrity and euphony for everyone, especially Leontes. Line continues, "Hermione's name also connects her with Hermes, who

---

172. Whereas the sheep-shearing festival, the center of Bohemia, opens with Autolycus singing a song of springtime.

in one form is the messenger of the gods and, in his higher form, the one who carries the word of God." [173]

In a reversal of her Part One intrusiveness, Paulina invites everyone into her home ... or is it her museum? ... or is it her chapel? In an earlier drama, another foolish protagonist gazed on a marble statue. When Othello entered Desdemona's bed chamber, carrying a single light, he might have wished he was entering a holy sepulcher containing a statue that could return to life: "Yet I'll not shed her blood/ Nor scar that whiter skin of hers than snow/ And smooth as monumental alabaster...." But Othello was doomed by some inner compulsion that greatly feared what he thought was Desdemona's sexual allure. So his "solution" was: "Yet she must die, else she'll betray more men./ Put out the light, and then put out the light" (5.2.3-7)!

Othello did not spend any years in prayer and contrition, but Leontes did. Polixenes is so struck with

---

173. Jill Line. *Shakespeare and The Ideal of Love*. Rochester, VT., Inner Traditions, 138.

the statue's verisimilitude that he declares, "The very life seems warm upon her lip." Looking at Leontes, Paulina thinks he is "transported," and Leontes admits to a "madness," but how different from his Act One madness. This madness is creative, not destructive:

Let no man mock me,
For I will kiss her. (5.3.79-80)

It is the kiss of life, more potent than any of Cleopatra's.[174] Does it not carry an echo of when "The Lord God also made the man of the dust of the ground, and breathed in his face breath of life, and the man was a living soul"? (Gen 2:7).

Paulina's chapel is also her theatre. Paulina's numinous incantation, quoted on page 4, above, begins, "It is requir'd/ You do awake your faith". She speaks purposefully: "it is required," reminding us that her name clearly carries ancestral seeds from St. Paul, the endorser of faith.[175] And at this moment, Paulina also banishes all witchcraft, at least from this play: "those

---

174. See Adelman, 164.
175. See, especially, Paul's Epistles to the Romans and First Corinthians.

that think it is unlawful business/ I am about, let them depart" (5.3.94-97)., but no one leaves. This marvelous scene *is* pure theatre, a word whose root is *thea,* "a sight," combined with *thauma,* "that which compels the gaze."[176] In this final scene, as magisterial Hermione descends from her death-in-life to embrace her husband but speak only with her daughter. Shakespeare, the stage's greatest *auteur,* so dazzles us that all we can do, as Paulina commands, is "all stand still" while we watch and listen to the rich chords of this heavenly theatre music.

■ *The Tempest*

> Be not afeard. The isle is full of noises,
> Sounds and sweet airs that give delight and hurt not.
> Sometimes a thousand twangling instruments
> Will hum about mine ears; and sometimes voices,
> That if I then had waked after long sleep,
> Will make me sleep again; and then in dreaming,
> The clouds, methought, would open and show riches
> Ready to drop upon me, that when I waked
> I cried to dream again.

---

176. From Erik Erikson's *Play and Development,* 137, as quoted by Schwartz, 198.

Why do you suppose Shakespeare gave these lines, the most beautiful in *The Tempest,* to the monster Caliban? How is it that only Caliban hears the music of the spheres on Prospero's island kingdom, that only Caliban affirms his honesty, "I do not lie," that only Caliban reveals Miranda's fecundity, "... she will become thy bed, I warrant,/ And bring thee forth brave brood," and only Caliban has penetrated to the secret of Prospero's power:

> First to possess his books, for without them
> He's but a sot, as I am ....? (3.2.92-3)

Is Prospero, then, just a Caliban with book-learning?

I have always thought that Prospero, while "the prime Duke" of Milan and "rapt in secret studies," stole off one day to Algiers for some R & R and there canoodled with the bewitching Sycorax, who undoubtedly introduced him to certain *erotica* known only to her. Their brief romantic interlude might have ended with a promise to rendezvous again, some fine day, on a lonely island between Naples and Tunis.[177] After all, in the final scene he comes clean and confesses, "this thing of darkness I/ Acknowledge mine." Is it not a patrilineal acknowledgement, or does Shakespeare have in mind something more interesting, more complex?

With those elegant nine lines is Shakespeare hinting that there is something admirable, perhaps even profound, in Caliban, even if hidden? In an April, 2005 Shakespeare Theatre of Washington (DC) production, during the masque scene (4.1), Miranda rises, leaves her place next to Ferdinand, and gently takes Caliban by the hand. For a brief minute or two, Beauty dances with the Beast who had tried to rape her. It was a deft touch by director Kate Whorjskey, acknowledging the rapid expansion of Miranda's moral compass. But how could this be? Miranda landed on this bare isle when she was but three years old. There were no seminaries, no universities, not even a market place where Miranda

---

177. Can we speculate, then, that Sycorax arrived too early, Prospero too late?

might engage in social conversation. Only her father and Caliban (and Ariel, whom she never sees). So what gave birth to her moral compass?

Clearly, the very careful home-schooling that Prospero spent twelve years inculcating upon his daughter and only heir:

> Here in this island we arrived, and here
> Have I, thy schoolmaster, made thee more profit
> Than other princes can that have more time
> For vainer hours, and tutors not so careful.
>   (1.2.171-4)

Miranda shows herself to be a worthy and complete young woman. Her very first words reveal that she knows her father is a wizard – "If by your art, my dearest father, you have/ Put the wild waters in this roar, allay them" (1.2.1-2). In the long dialogue between father and daughter that is 1.2, we see Miranda as compassionate, curious, bright, articulate, and with a pert sense of humor. We shall soon see her also as passionate. Prospero had twelve years to tutor her carefully, tutor her himself, not like "other princes." His purpose clearly was not to enable his daughter to become a better island citizen but to unite the kingdoms of Milan and Naples, via Miranda and Ferdinand, and to assure himself that his progeny would be noble and worthy.

Act One, Scene Two, is a long and crucial one – 502 lines. First we learn how Prospero and Miranda came to be exiled – a *Hamlet* story sans Gertrude:

> I thus neglecting worldly ends ...
> in my false brother
> Awaked an evil nature, and my trust,
> Like a good parent, did beget of him
> A falsehood in its contrary as great
> As my trust was, which had indeed no limit,
> A confidence sans bound. (1.2.89-97)

Despite his misplaced trust in his brother, Prospero did not lose the capacity or the desire for trust but wisely transferred all of his to Miranda. Love and trust for this father-daughter duo seems inborn and not something they had to struggle to attain. In this scene we also meet Ariel, Caliban, and Ferdinand for the first time, and the two young people dazzle each other – Romeo and Juliet without street brawls and warring families, though not without monarchial and personal conflicts in the background. Immediately, Ferdinand is tested thrice: does he appreciate music, does he admire Miranda, and is he brave enough to challenge Prospero. He easily passes all three challenges, as he will later endure the physical and demeaning charge of transporting large, heavy logs.[178]

And the two young people? "At the first sight/ They have changed eyes" (1.2.441-442). Miranda calls him a god; Ferdinand calls her a goddess. As Prospero says to us, "It works." How ironic that Prospero chooses for his daughter the son of his inveterate enemy, emblematic of the great paradox that is life. This first step in the reconciliation of the kingdoms of Milan and Naples shadows the marriage of Claribel, Alonso's daughter, to the King of Tunis. Her marriage united two continents and two races. Line 16, spoken by Prospero, is key: "I have done nothing but in care of thee...." Shakespeare is still dealing with witches and witchcraft

---

178. Perhaps a faint echo of the labors of Hercules, or of Caliban's labors.

and father-son relationships, but now, in his last solo drama, he focuses primarily on the father-daughter bond.

In Chapter One, above, the daughter, Joan, more than mishandles her father. She simply denies he was hers. From James's viewpoint, she deserves the death the English gave her, bound to a burning picket. In Chapter Two, Juliet's harsh father acts in the conventional Elizabethan fashion: "Marry whom I choose for you or you're out on the street." In *Midsummer,* Hermia's father, Egeus, brings the same complaint to the Duke, but the spirit of the forest, where Oberon and Titania and their minions cavort all night long, soon mitigates Egeus's wrath. In *The Merchant of Venice,* the dead father is obeyed *to the letter;* the live one abandoned wholesale. So, in a complex sort of way, we might say that in Shakespeare's Venetian tale the father-daughter duel is a draw.

In Chapter Three, fathers and daughters have disappeared, only to come roaring back in Chapter Four, in the so-called High Tragedies. In *Hamlet,* Ophelia's father ruins her chances with the crown prince by interdicting their social and romantic intercourse. Whenever there is no mother and only one daughter, one has to ponder the possibility of incest. Polonius was glad enough to send Laertes back to Paris, leaving him and Ophelia the solo occupants of his hearth. In a Shakespeare & Company (Lenox, MA) production on August 26, 2009, Polonius's words and body language at the end of 2.1 made the thought of incest manifest. When Ophelia movingly tells him that, in essence, she saw a ghost – "Lord Hamlet, with his doublet all unbrac'd,/ ...Pale as his shirt .../ As if he had been loosed out of hell...." --- Polonius's immediate reaction is "Mad for thy love?" Director Eleanor Holdridge portrayed Polonius as a dirty old man, another Pandarus: "I fear'd he did but trifle/ And meant to wrack thee. But beshrew my jealousy!" And then, when her father is killed, because he espied one time too many, Ophelia comes undone.

Father-daughter in *Othello* is less clear. Once again, we have no mother and only a daughter in residence. Why would Desdemona, whom I picture as older than Juliet but certainly younger than Cleopatra, leave her senator-father's house and elope with a much older stranger (even forgetting that he was a Moor)? Was it was simply time to go; she's ready for marriage? Brabantio accused Othello of employing "spells and medicines bought of mountebanks," of witchcraft, and "practices of cunning hell." All of which turned out to be Othello's tales of his many odysseys which Desdemona "with a greedy ear [would] devour." Brabantio, like Polixenes, was not consulted, and the ties that bind Desdemona to Othello become undone on Cyprus after she leaves her father and their bond behind in Venice.

In *King Lear,* in one fell swoop Lear lays the groundwork for disastrous liaisons with all three daughters. To Goneril and Regan he gives too much while they too eagerly pander to his old man's demand for honey-praise. He brutally dismisses Cordelia who speaks a truth he will not hear. The price he pays is high as he becomes homeless in his own kingdom and must endure the hell of two raging storms, one outer and one inner. It's a Dantean journey from hell to purgatory and only at the end to some heavenly vision with his one true daughter, now dead in his lap, *pieta*. As A.C. Bradley so beautifully described it, his "sight is so purged by scalding tears that it sees at last how power and place and all things in the world are vanity except love...."[179]

In *The Winter's Tale,* King Leontes came very close to tossing his new-born daughter into the flames, so fiery was his self-inflicted jealousy. His disease kills his only son, who languishes unto death when his mother is jailed. Only Paulina's steadfast faith, Florizel's unflinching love, and Perdita's earthy ardor redeem Leontes, who has to suffer through sixteen years of prayer and contrition.

But, at the end of Shakespeare's dramatic career, Prospero gets the father-daughter consanguinity right. The catalytic action of the plot takes place before the curtain rises. We learn some of the details in 1.2, as Prospero tells Miranda, "The hour's now come" to hear

---

179. A.C. Bradley, *Shakespearean Tragedy*. London, Macmillan (1937), 285.

their history. And what a tale it is, of Prospero's love for his books, of brotherly treachery, of being put to sea in a "rotten carcass of a butt," and of "bountiful fortune." There is no mistaking that this father-daughter tale will be beneficent the minute we hear Prospero tell his daughter, "I have done nothing but in care of thee." Before he can test Ferdinand, Prospero is himself first tested, at sea, to be father, mother, and ladies-in-waiting to Miranda. "Alack," she declares, "what trouble/ Was I then to you?" But his response is telling: "O, a cherubin/ Thou wast that did preserve me." As the Arden edition footnote makes clear, she was, literally, his life preserver, saving "him from spiritual despair and hence, presumably, from death at sea." So Miranda saves him from despair at sea while, later, Ariel saves him from *hubris* on land.

Of all the father-daughter connections so briefly discussed in this essay, the one that seems closest to Prospero-Miranda is Lear-Cordelia.[180] Perhaps at night,

---

180. Curiously, Miranda and Cordelia speak virtually the same number of lines, 112 and 114, respectively.

in the silence of his study, after all the crowds had left

The Globe, Shakespeare himself fell in love with Lear

and Cordelia at the end:

Cordelia: Shall we not see these daughters and these
sisters?

Lear: No, no, no, no. Come, let's away to prison;
We two alone will sing like birds i' the cage.
When thou dost ask me blessing I'll kneel
down
And ask of thee forgiveness. So we'll live
And pray, and sing, and tell tall tales ...
And take upon's the mystery of things
As if we were God's spies. And we'll wear out
In a walled prison packs and sects of great
ones
That ebb and flow by the moon. (5.3.7-19)

But Lear brought his agonies on himself by his imperious

and high-handed actions at the drama's inception. So

perhaps Shakespeare was eager to create a father both

wise and loving, even though he knew that his magic

kingdom island could not escape the ills of the "history

of the world… [consisting] of a struggle for power … [including] murder, revolt and violence."[181]

The real brilliance of *The Tempest* is encapsulated in that key line from 1.2. Here is Prospero's complete speech:

> I have done nothing but in care of thee,
> Of thee, my dear one, thee my daughter, who
> Art ignorant of what thou art, naught knowing
> Of whence I am, nor that I am more better
> Than Prospero, master of a full poor cell,
> And thy no greater father. (1.2.16-21)

The speech is suffused with deeply felt fatherly love as well as prefatory hints of what Prospero has in mind for Miranda and for the future of his family and his regime, once reinstated as Duke of Milan. To borrow a phrase uttered by Prospero's thuggish brother, "What's past is prologue, what to come/ In yours and my discharge" (2.1.253-254). Prospero's major task in life is to find Miranda a worthy husband and prepare for the next generation. His entire purpose in raising the storm

181. Ian Kott. *Shakespeare Our Contemporary*. New York, Norton (1974), 309.

is to bring Ferdinand to the island, have him and Miranda meet, and determine whether Ferdinand is worthy to take his daughter away from him.

But along with Ferdinand come all the other Europeans on the ship.[182] What was Prospero to do with them, especially since some of them were his enemies, some were assassins-*manqués*, and others just drunken louts? In brief, they represented everything Shakespeare knew about life at court – intrigue, ambition, murderous inclinations, regicide, fratricide, usurpation, drunkenness, and – thankfully – kindness, in the person of Gonzalo.[183] With one hand he decided to test Ferdinand. With the other he determined to show off his magical powers, everything he had learned from his studies in Milan and which, ironically, was the proximate cause of his expulsion. Did he want revenge? Well, yes, of a sort, but he did not intend to kill his enemies, just to frighten them, to show off, and play what he called

---

182. Also along came Caliban, and some commentators have written that whatever incestuous impulse Prospero might have entertained is deflected onto Caliban, where, in this play, it more properly belongs.
183. Is the island Elsinore in mid-sea?

"tricks." Along the way, Prospero himself learned the great lesson of his life, thanks to Ariel, the creative spirit within him:

> Though with their high wrongs I am struck to th'
>   quick,
> Yet with my nobler reason 'gainst my fury
> Do I take part. The rarer action is
> In virtue than in vengeance. They being penitent,
> The sole drift of my purpose doth extend
> Not a frown further. Go, release them, Ariel,
> My charms I'll break; their senses I'll restore;
> And they shall be themselves. (5.1.25-32)

"And they shall be themselves," no longer his prisoners. Prospero's passion becomes compassion.[184] The true risk Prospero runs is not really the plot against his life; a few tawdry costumes flapping on the clothesline avert that. Rather, he is tempted by *hubris,* tempted to believe that just because "graves at my command/ Have waked their sleepers, ope'd and let 'em forth," his "so potent art" placed him next to the gods, and he deserved to be immune to "the whips and scorns of time."

---

184. For this phrase and some of the Epilogue discussion I am indebted to a talk by Helen Luke, privately given me by Mary Burns of Taos, NM.

In some mysterious fashion, his "trickster," Ariel, gently leads him away from *hubris:*

Ariel: Your charm so strongly works 'em
That, if you now beheld them, your affections
Would become tender.

Prospero: Dost thou think so, spirit?

Ariel: Mine would, sir, were I human.

Prospero: --And mine shall. (5.1.17-20)

"Were I human." Is Ariel not human? Prospero calls her a "spirit." The spirit of what? Although she is willing (mostly) to do Prospero's bidding, her overarching desire is to regain her freedom, just like Caliban. And, in the end, Prospero grants freedom to them both, not without regret: "My dainty Ariel! I shall miss thee,/ But yet thou shalt have freedom" (5.1.95-96). It's the right thing to do.

End of play? Not quite yet, for there's an Epilogue, and this one, unlike all others in the canon, is spoken by the protagonist, by Prospero himself. "Please you, draw near," he urges the audience.[185] On one level the Epilogue is the traditional plea for applause, but that is not its essence. Prospero has already told us that soon "Every third thought shall be my grave." So the Epilogue represents the final thoughts of an older, highly creative man who has just set in motion his heart's desire for his daughter, for the next generation, and for the future of his regime. It has been a virtuous voyage, and now he asks the audience, all those unseen people on the other side of the footlights, to set *him* free. Since he has "pardoned the deceiver" and his "charms are all o'erthrown," he asks his audience (and that includes you and me) to pray for him, pray so deeply as to "assault mercy itself," that is, entreat for divine grace. It is the same "mercy" that Portia preached in court. We pray that he not remain on the bare island, now no longer peopled and where his ending would be despair, but be freed to return to Naples where he can watch Ferdinand, to whom he has given "a third of mine own life," wed

---

185. Yes, I know the script claims he says this to his "guests," but in reality he says this to us.

Miranda, who, he tells her future husband, "thou shalt find she will outstrip all praise/ And make it halt behind her" (4.1.3, 10-11).

I close with this message from John Ashbery's *Notes from the Air*:

> ...No more trivia, please, but music
> in all the spheres, leading up to where the
> master wants to talk to you,
> place his mouth over yours,
> withdraw the human fishhook from the
>   crystalline flesh
> where it was melting, give you back your
>   clothes, penknife, twine.
> And where shall we go when we leave?

❖

WORKS CONSULTED

Works by Shakespeare:

David Bevington, ed. *The Arden Shakespeare Troilus and Cressida.* London: Thomson, 2006.

Wolfgang Clemen, ed. *A Midsummer Night's Dream.* New York: Signet Classics, 1998.

Barbara Everett, ed. *The Tragedy of Antony and Cleopatra.* New York: Signet Classics, 1988.

R.A. Foakes, ed. *The Arden Shakespeare King Lear.* London: Thomson, 2007.

Brian Gibbons, ed. *The Arden Shakespeare Romeo and Juliet.* London: Thomson Learning, 1980.

Stephen Greenblatt, ed. *The Norton Shakespeare Tragedies.* New York: Norton. 1997.

E.A.J. Honigmann, ed. *The Arden Shakespeare Othello.* London: Thomson, 2006.

Harold Jenkins, ed. *The Arden Shakespeare Hamlet.* London: Thomson, 2001.

George Lyman Kittredge, ed. *The Tragedy of Hamlet.* Boston: Ginn, 1939.

Barbara A. Mowat and Paul Werstine, eds. *Folger Shakespeare Library The Merchant of Venice.* New York: Washington Square, 1992.

_____, eds. *Folger Shakespeare Library Shakespeare's Sonnets and Poems.* New York: Washington Square, 2006.

Kenneth Muir, ed. *The Arden Shakespeare Macbeth.* London: Thomson, 2006.

J.H.P. Pafford, ed. *The Arden Shakespeare The Winter's Tale.* London: Thomson, 2006.

Lawrence V. Ryan, ed. *Henry VI, Part One.* New York: Signet Classics, 2005.

Virginia Mason Vaughan and Alden T. Vaughan, eds. *The Arden Shakespeare The Tempest.* London: Thomson, 2000.

Works by others:

Absher, Tom. *Men and The Goddess: Feminine Archetypes in Western Literature.* Rochester, VT: Park St. Press, 1990.

Adelman, Janet. *The Common Liar.* New Haven: Yale Press, 1973.

Barker, Deborah and Ivo Kamps, eds. *Shakespeare and Gender.* London: Verso, 1995.

Bate, Jonathan. *Soul of the Age.* New York: Random House, 2009.

Bate, W.J. ed. *Criticism: The Major Texts.* New York: Harcourt Brace, 1952.

Bloom, Harold. *Shakespeare: The Invention of the Human.* New York: Penguin, 1998.

Bradley, A.C. *Shakespearean Tragedy.* London: 1937.

Carney, Jo Eldridge. *Fairy Tale Queens.* New York: Paul Grave, 2012.

Di Matteo, Anthony. "'*Antiqui dicunt':* classical aspects of the witches in 'Macbeth.'" *Notes and Queries.* 41.1 (March, 1944).

Fiedler, Leslie A. *The Stranger in Shakespeare.* New York: Barnes & Noble, 2006.

Fisher, Philip. "Thinking about Killing: Hamlet and the Paths among the Passions." Raritan X (Summer, 1991).

French, Marilyn. *Shakespeare's Division of Experience.* New York: Summit Books, 1981.

Frye, Northrop. *Anatomy of Criticism.* Princeton: PU Press, 1990.

1599 Geneva Bible. White Hall, WV: Tolle Lege, 2006.

Greenblatt, Stephen, "The Death of Hamnet and the Making of Hamlet." *The New York Review of Books* LI. 16 (October 21, 2004).

_____, *Hamlet in Purgatory.* Princeton: PU Press, 2001.

Hodgdon, Barbara. *The End Crowns All: Closure and Contradiction in Shakespeare's History.* Princeton: PU Press, 1991.

Hughes, Paul H. and James F. Larkin. *Tudor Royal Proclamations, Vol. II.* New Haven: Yale UP, 1969.

Janouch, Gustav. *Conversations with Franz Kafka.* New York: New Directions (1971).

Kahn, Coppélia. *Man's Estate: Masculine Identity in Shakespeare.* Berkeley: UC Press, 1981.

Kott, Ian. *Shakespeare Our Contemporary.* New York: Norton, 1974.

Lahr, John. "Majestic Moor." *The New Yorker,* January 21, 2008.

Levin, Carole. "'Murder Not Then the Fruit Within My Womb': Shakespeare's Joan, Foxe's Guernsey Martyr, and Women Pleading Pregnancy in Early Modern English History and Culture." *Quidditas: Journal of the Rocky Mountain Renaissance Association.* 20 (1999).

_____. *The Reign of Elizabeth I.* New York: Palgrave, 2002.

Lewalski, Barbara. "Biblical Allusion and Allegory in *The Merchant of Venice.*" *Shakespeare Quarterly* 13.3 (Summer 1962).

Line, Jill. *Shakespeare and the Ideal of Love.* Rochester, VT: Inner Traditions, 2004.

Marlowe, Christopher. *Doctor Faustus.* Ed. Sylvan Barnet. New York: Signet Classics, 2001.

Merriam, Thomas. "Faustian Joan." *Notes and Queries.* 49.2 (June 2002).

Midgley, Graham. "The Merchant of Venice: A reconsideration." *Essays in Criticism 10* (April 1960).

Muir, Kenneth, ed. *Shakespeare: The Comedies.* Englewood Cliffs: Prentice-Hall, 1965.

Ovid, *Metamorphoses.* Tr. David Raeburn. London: Penguin, 2004.

Rackin, Phyllis, "Anti-Historians: Women's Roles in Shakespeare's Histories." *Theatre Journal.* 37.3, 1985.

Schwartz, Murray M. "Leontes' Jealousy in *The Winter's Tale.*" *American Imago* 30.3 (Fall, 1973), 250-273.

_____. *"The Winter's Tale:* Loss and Transformation." *American Imago* 32.2 (Summer, 1975), 145-199.

Tillyard, E.M.W. *Shakespeare's Last Plays.* New York: Barnes and Noble, 1968.

Tricomi, Albert H. "Joan La Pucelle and the Inverted Saints Play in *1 Henry VI.*" *Renaissance and Reformation XXV,* 2 (2001).

Walker, Julia M., ed. *Dissing Elizabeth: Negative Representations of Gloriana.* Durham: Duke Press, 1998.

Wheeler, Richard P. *Shakespeare's Development and the Problem Comedies.* Los Angeles: UC Press, 1981.

APPENDICES

■ Appendix A: Chronology

I have used Harold Bloom's Chronology from his *Shakespeare: The Invention of the Human* and interspersed a few important biographical dates from a Folger Library publication.

April 26, 1564, Shakespeare christened at Stratford-on-Avon

Henry VI, Part One	**1589-90**
Henry VI, Part Two	**1590-91**
Henry VI, Part Three	**1590-91**
Richard III	**1592-93**
The Two Gentlemen of Verona	**1592-93**
Hamlet (first version)	**1589-93**
Venus and Adonis	**1592-93**
The Comedy of Errors	**1593**

Sonnets	**1593-1609**
The Rape of Lucrece	**1593-94**
Titus Andronicus	**1593-94**
The Taming of the Shrew	**1593-94**

1594 Shakespeare becomes a share owner in the Lord Chamberlin's company

Love's Labour's Lost	**1594-95**
King John	**1594-96**
Richard II	**1595**
Romeo and Juliet	**1595-96**
A Midsummer Night's Dream	**1595-96**

1596 Hamnet dies. Grant of arms to Shakespeare's father.

The Merchant of Venice	**1596-97**
Henry IV, Part One	**1596-97**
The Merry Wives of Windsor	**1597**

May 4, 1597, Purchase of New Place, Stratford-on-Avon.

Henry IV, Part Two	1598
Much Ado About Nothing	1598-99
Henry V	1599
Julius Caesar	1599
As You Like It	1599

1599 Opening of the Globe Theater.

Hamlet	1600-1601
The Phoenix and The Turtle	1601

September 8, 1601, burial of Shakespeare's father.

Twelfth Night	1601-02
Troilus and Cressida	1601-02
All's Well That Ends Well	1602-03
Measure for Measure	1604
Othello	1604

King Lear	1605
Macbeth	1606
Antony and Cleopatra	1606
Coriolanus	1607-08
Timon of Athens	1607-08
Pericles	1607-08

September 9, 1608, burial of Shakespeare's mother.

Cymbeline	1609-1610
The Winter's Tale	1610-11
The Tempest	1611
A Funeral Elegy	1612
Henry VIII	1612-13
The Two Noble Kinsmen	1613

April 23, 1616, Shakespeare died at Stratford-upon-Avon.

Appendix B: Songs

Shakespeare loved music, and we can hear songs – literally and metaphorically -- in many of his plays. Music frequently announces happiness or good fortune. In the three casket scene of *The Merchant of Venice,* only for suitor Bassanio does Portia request, "Let music sound while he doth make his choice" (3.2.43), just in case we didn't already know Bassanio would win the contest for her hand (and fortune). In contrast, Ophelia's sad songs, like "How should I your true love know...?", accompany the slow, wrenching, unraveling of her young, disappointed mind (in 4.5).

Perhaps Shakespeare expressed his own view in Lorenzo's mini-lecture to Jessica, his fiancée, near the end of *Merchant.* The lovers are safely housed on Belmont, awaiting Portia's return to her island of song and romance, when Lorenzo asks for music, describing for Jessica the music of the spheres, the "harmony [which] is in immoral souls ... [that] we cannot hear...." Expressing the only discordant note in their courtship,

Jessica tells him, "I am never merry when I hear sweet music." Wanting nothing to interfere with their immanent consummation, for eighteen lines Lorenzo turns schoolmaster, clearly drawing the moral:

The man that hath no music in himself,
Nor is moved with concord of sweet sounds,
Is fit for treasons, stratagems, and spoils;
The motions of his spirit are dull as night,
And his affections dark as Erebus.
Let no such man be trusted. Mark the music.
                    (5.1.83-8)

As I assembled this essay, certain popular songs crept into my head. I saw them as appropriate to the subject matter and as a kind of background tribute to the great English playwright. Many celebrated classical composers have used his plays as inspiration – Mendelssohn's charming overture to *A Midsummer Night's Dream* perhaps the best-known example. My modest effort is derivative, not creative. [186]

---

[186]For every song and ballad sung in the plays as well as others alluded to, see Ross W. Duffin, 186. *Shakespeare's Songbook* (Norton, 2004). Also Frederick W. Sternfeld, *Songs From Shakespeare's Tragedies* (Oxford, 1964) and *Music in Shakespearian Tragedy* (1963).

Here are my notes on choosing which songs for which chapters. My, how Shakespeare would have loved all of these!

Introduction: "Fascinating Rhythm": Written for the 1924 musical *Lady Be Good,* this song is one of the best efforts by the Gershwin brothers:

> Each morning I get up with the sun ...
> To find at night no work has been done....
> Oh, how I long to be the man I used to be!
> Fascinating rhythm,
> Oh won't you stop picking on me?

Chapter One: "That's Why the Lady is a Tramp": From the 1937 musical *Babes in Arms,* music by that great genius Richard Rodgers and his first genius partner, Lorenz Hart:

> I've wined and dined on Mulligan stew
> And never wished for turkey...
> Don't know the reason for cocktails at five...
> I crave affection, but not when I drive ...
> That's why the lady is a tramp.

Chapter Two: "You Do Something to Me": Written in 1929 by the remarkable Cole Porter for his first integrated-book musical, *Fifty Million Frenchmen*:

> You do something to me,
> Something that simply mystifies me.
> Tell me, why should it be
> You have the power to hypnotize me….
> Let me live 'neath your spell,
> Do do that voodoo
> That you do so well.
> For you do something to me
> That nobody else could do!

Chapter Three: "They Didn't Believe Me": In 1914 Jerome Kern teamed with lyricist Herbert Reynolds in the musical *The Girl from Utah*. She must have been some babe:

> And when I told them how beautiful you are,
> They didn't believe me. They didn't believe me!
> Your lips, your eyes, your cheeks, your hair,
> Are in a class beyond compare. …
> And when I tell them,
> And I cert'nly am goin' to tell them,
> That I'm the man whose wife one day you'll be.
> They'll never believe me. They'll never believe me.
> That from this great big world you've chosen me!

Chapter Four: "My Funny Valentine": Another illustrious tune from Rodgers and Hart's *Babes in Arms.* It became immensely popular in the year following the show, recorded by more than 600 artists on more than 1300 albums. Everyone remembers the Frank Sinatra and Ella Fitzgerald renditions, but how many of you know Mabel Mercer's?

> My funny Valentine
> Sweet comic Valentine
> You make me smile with my heart
> Your looks are laughable, unphotographable
> Yet you're my favorite work of art….
> But don't change a hair for me
> Not if you care for me
> Stay little Valentine stay
> Each day is Valentine's Day.

Chapter Five: "I'll Be Seeing You": Sammy Fain and lyricist Irving Kahal's 1938 musical *Right This Way* was a dismal failure, closing after only fifteen performances. Its signature song lives on:

> I'll be seeing you
> In all the old familiar places

That this heart of mine embraces
All day through….

I'll find you in the morning sun
And when the night is new.
I'll be looking at the moon,
But I'll be seeing you.

Not for the proud man apart
From the raging moon I write
On these spindrift pages
Nor for the towering dead
With their nightingales and psalms
But for the lovers, their arms
Round the griefs of the ages,
Who pay no praise or wages
Nor heed my craft or art.

Dylan Thomas